THE
POSTMODERNIST
TURN

TWAYNE'S AMERICAN THOUGHT AND CULTURE SERIES

Lewis Perry, General Editor

THE POSTMODERNIST TURN

American Thought and Culture in the 1970s

J. DAVID HOEVELER, JR.

Twayne Publishers
An Imprint of Simon & Schuster Macmillan
New York

Prentice Hall International
London • Mexico City • New Delhi • Singapore • Sydney • Toronto

The Postmodernist Turn: American Thought and Culture in the 1970s
J. David Hoeveler, Jr.

Copyright © 1996 by J. David Hoeveler, Jr.

Twayne Publishers
An Imprint of Simon & Schuster Macmillan
1633 Broadway
New York, New York 10019

Library of Congress Cataloging-in-Publication Data
Hoeveler, J. David, 1943–
     The Postmodernist Turn : American thought and culture in the 1970s /
J. David Hoeveler
        p.   cm. — (Twayne's American thought and culture series)
     Includes bibliographical references and index.
     ISBN 0-8057-9064-0 (cloth)
     1. United States—Civilization—1970– 2. United States—
Intellectual life—20th century.   3. Nineteen seventies.
     4. Postmodernism—United States.   I. Perry, Lewis, 1938–
     II. Title.   III. Series.
E169.12.H6   1996
973.924—dc20   96-28257
                                                                 CIP

The paper used in this publication meets the minimum requirements of American National Standard for Information Sciences—Permanence of Paper for Printed Library Materials. ANSI Z39.48–1984. ∞ ™

10 9 8 7 6 5 4 3 2 1

Printed in the United States of America

This book is for Emily

Contents

Contents

Illustrations

Foreword

The American Thought and Culture Series surveys intellectual and cultural life in America from the sixteenth century to the present. The time is auspicious for such a broad survey because scholars have carried out so much pathbreaking work in this field in recent years. The volumes reflect that scholarship as well as valuable earlier studies. The authors also present the results of their own research and offer original interpretations. The goal is to bring together books that are readable and well informed and that stand on their own as introductions to significant periods in American thought and culture. There is no attempt to establish a single interpretation of all of America's past; the diversity, conflict, and change that are features of the American experience would frustrate any such attempt. What the authors can do, however, is to explore issues that are of critical importance to both a particular period and the whole of American history.

Today the culture and intellectual life of the United States are subjects of heated debate. While prominent figures summon citizens back to an endangered "common culture," some critics dismiss the very idea of culture—let alone American culture—as elitist and arbitrary. The questions asked in these volumes are directly relevant to that debate, which concerns history but too often proceeds in ignorance of it. How did leading intellectuals view their relations to America, and how did their compatriots regard them? Did Americans believe that theirs was a distinctive culture? Did they participate in international movements? What were the links and tensions between high culture and popular culture? While discussing influential works, creative individuals, and major institutions, the books in this series place intellectual and cultural history in the larger context of American society.

David Hoeveler's volume examines a recent decade: the 1970s. Some of the images he presents may seem strikingly contemporary: jobs vanishing overseas, old certainties imperiled by "future shock," widespread anxiety about creature comforts and personal health. *The Postmodernist Turn* demonstrates that analyses of the decline of industrial society have been in circulation since at least the 1970s and that many writers influential in the late 1990s began to refocus debate within their fields a quarter century before. Professor Hoeveler stresses that the 1970s were a decade of transition, and the vantage point of the 1990s enables him to detect the direction in which change was turning. As the practical and political allegiances of the 1960s and earlier decades disintegrated, intellectuals often turned toward academic theory and abstraction. Thus, Hoeveler concentrates on movements defined by "coming afterward"—*post*industrialism and *post*modernism. In the 1970s some writers claimed that intellectual elites were more important than they had ever been before; yet, within elite circles, others challenged the very foundations of knowledge and questioned whether knowledge can ever be about anything other than the words it is expressed in, whether the production of knowledge was anything more than a game to be played. In exploring the creative life of the 1970s, Hoeveler does not present change as irresistible or ignore the confrontational and oppositional. He examines a wide range of topics, including movements to release painting and architecture from modernist orthodoxy, debates over what was essential and what was historical and changing in African-American life, the retreat (or advance) of Marxism into the corridors of postmodernist theorizing, new voices in feminism as an intellectual and academic profession, redefinitions and restored confidence in conservatism, and sharply different endeavors to reinvigorate liberalism.

The Postmodernist Turn not only charts historical change in a decade of the recent past. It accomplishes what some of Hoeveler's subjects doubted was ever really possible in historical study: it helps us to understand the intellectual landscape in which we find ourselves several decades later.

LEWIS PERRY
Series Editor

Preface

The 1970s seem to lie in American memory as a nondescript interlude. Caught between the sixties of infamy and the eighties of ill repute, it bears that most banal of descriptions, a "transitional era." Perhaps that generality holds because we still tend to measure our history by political change, and to that extent the transition label gains some plausibility. In 1972, the residual power of 1960s reform and protest had enough suasion in the Democratic party to give the presidential nomination to the most avowedly leftist candidate that party had chosen in the twentieth century, George McGovern. By the end of the decade, in contrast, the Republicans were ready to choose their most emphatically conservative nominee in this century, Ronald Reagan. In between lay the mild conservatism of Gerald Ford and the moderate liberalism of Jimmy Carter. "Transition" thus seems apt enough.

But the 1970s has yet to win an identity of its own. As one who follows the new American history textbooks that appear on the market, I have not yet seen an effort to bracket this decade in a way that will cause it to resonate like "the Twenties," "the Thirties," "the Fifties," and even "the Eighties," have done. These decades convey particular symbols and images that personify or label them. I hope this book will help. My focus, as this book's place in a series indicates, is thought and culture. I will try to show that at least within these subfields, the 1970s made a significant turn and not merely a transitional one. Of course, it built on movements underway before the 70s, and the fullest implications of intellectual change in the 1970s became more largely fulfilled later. However, the 1970s did bring American thought and culture into a new era.

To make this point, I present this book as an extended essay. I appreciate the editor's guidelines to this series' authors not to write a comprehensive history of their respective chronological periods. I do not pretend to have done so in any way. Even within the categories of thought and culture that I have selected for consideration, I have not tried to review all events or noted all individuals who would be significant or interesting for a more inclusive treatment of these subjects. Instead, I have tried to highlight major developments that cut across the categories of thought and culture. I have tried to identify directions or redefinitions that appear, for example, in literary criticism, with similar ones in philosophy or architecture. Reading across these subjects increasingly reinforced my sense that the 1970s was making significant shifts and approaching a new paradigm that became emblematic of the decade. Within these shifts, I believe, the 1970s makes its permanent contribution to American thought and culture. I have described the seventies under the general heading of "postmodernism."

Postmodernism found its way gradually and uncertainly into academic discourse in the 1970s. Some of its outlines and rhetorical devices were in use even before the label appeared as a descriptive device. Important writings by Susan Sontag in the 1960s, for example, anticipated postmodernism, though she did not employ that term.[1] Literary critic Leslie Fiedler had begun to use the term postmodern in the 1950s and linked it to a partisan cause against modernism. His writing joined the postmodernist idea to a radical politics poised against all the norms of bourgeois humanism.[2] Then in the early 1970s Ihab Hassan used the term postmodernism and helped create the debate, soon joined by many parties, about its meanings.[3]

Although I construct the book as an extended thematic essay, it would defy the main theme itself to present the '70s in terms of some rigid superstructure or "metanarrative," as the poststructuralists would say. Indeed, that term expresses almost everything that the postmodernist shift sought to undermine and invalidate. The recurring motif in 1970s culture is the dismantling of inherited forms, descriptive norms, sharp and inclusive modes of categorization; instead, we have the blurring of distinctions, the mixing of forms, a discomfort with preciseness in signification and representation. The 1970s moved toward a culture of "post-" and "neo-": postmodernism, poststructuralism, neoconser- vatism, postphilosophy, neo-Marxism. The 1970s arrived to its place of recognition in American intellectual history by a series of undermining acts; it often had to define its common enterprise by subversive strategies, sometimes by negations. The 1970s, it seems, did not aspire to replace older inclusive wholes by new ones. It disassembled in order to begin anew or to pick and choose from the past.

This conclusion may seem troubling and inadequate and even a basis of criticism of the 1970s. But the judgment that the '70s moved into a nether world of "after everything" and left no legacy save radical skepticism misleads, I believe. I hope the reader will find it appropriate that the last chapter ends with philosophy and a discussion of pragmatism. I believe that this turn in philosophy speaks for the general direction taken by 1970s culture in a recovery of a classic norm of American intellectual life. The postmodernist shift signified a new opening to pragmatism. The Americans in this book thus significantly domesticated the more radical intellectual movements emanating from Europe. What emerged was something that could appear radically new, and often disturbing in American life, but that, upon closer consideration, may be seen to have regenerated older habits and progressive forces in the American tradition.

Some of the material will be new and strange to the general reader. I should say a few words about that. First, I believe that the important clues to the 1970s may be discerned in close and careful attention to matters seemingly recondite and abstract. I have sought out those clues. Second, although my experience in teaching confirms that many students approach items like "deconstruction" or "poststructuralism" with intimidation, I have also found that they can write and think well about them and that they ultimately find them more engaging than they expected. Third, I give attention to these subjects because they transcend narrow academic concerns and readily enter the realm of more familiar political discourse. I have focused on the "political" readings of literary criticism and other subjects to show that these "esoteric" subjects have a larger applicable interest for the intellectual history of the 1970s.

The first chapter gives an economic grounding for the intellectual changes discussed in the book. Postindustrialism describes not only major shifts in American economic life, ones that emerged prevalently in the 1970s, but new directions in social culture, too. One should not be reductive about relating postindustrialism to postmodernism, but the history of the 1970s, broadly considered, certainly points to a symbiosis that helps us understand each.

MILWAUKEE
May 1996

Acknowledgements

I am grateful to the Center for Twentieth Century Studies at the University of Wisconsin-Milwaukee for a full fellowship appointment in 1988–1989. There is no better place to be absorbed in matters cultural, critical, and theoretical and I thank my colleagues there for a year of intellectual stimulation. I am thankful to this university for the sabbatical leave I enjoyed in 1993–1994, which I used to complete the first writing for this book.

I also want to thank People's Books, a wonderful little bookstore on the East Side of Milwaukee that stocks an incredible array of items on delightfully esoteric subjects.

Lewis Perry, editor of this series, has provided me excellent advice and assistance. I am most grateful to him.

I owe particular thanks to my wife Diane, Professor of English at Marquette University. She introduced me to the great theoretical debates in literary criticism and got me interested in them. She has guided me though this wilderness.

This book is dedicated to our daughter Emily, now twelve years old. She is the brightest smile in my life.

one

Postindustrialism

It was a silent revolution. It stormed no barricades. It imposed no new ideology on the political order. Often it was barely visible on the landscape. None knew exactly how to mark its beginnings on history's time lines. But there was no mistaking that postindustrialism was changing the fabric of American life, from the specific way people earned their living to the less definable "feel" of things in the late twentieth century. Postindustrialism offered a field day of speculation to sociologists and prognosticators of all kinds. And it seemed clearly to be redefining American cultural life. How precisely it was doing so brought no consensus, but tackling that question yielded a suggestive and intriguing literature about where we were and where we were headed.

The term "postindustrial" gained wide currency in the 1970s. It served primarily to explain prominent changes in the American economy. It marked what many observers called the third century of American economic life. The industrial era that followed the preindustrial era seemed to have lasted but little more than a century and now the United States was entering its postindustrial age.[1]

The prior industrial economy, it was said, centered in the production of goods. Manufacturing constituted the critical sector of the economy. It determined the location of related business activity and forged the dominant culture of the working classes. The rhythm of life followed the timetable of machinery. It responded to the demands for synchronization of all component parts of the industrial process. At the turn of the century, Thorstein Veblen had given a brilliant descriptive account of the new machine order and its cultural incidents in his book *The Theory of Business Enterprise*. He described the imposing rationality of the industrial system, the "discipline" of the machine process and the standardization of all its components. Each reinforced the other and absorbed them into its operations. Veblen observed that individuals acquired a matter-of-fact habit of thinking as the machine process reshaped all aspects of daily life.

The industrial economy had induced major geographical shifts in the American population.[2] Vast numbers of people moved to the cities and metropolitan locations housed most of the population by 1950. Attending the shifts were the social phenomena we have come to associate with modern life—the decay of tribal society with its traditional controls, increased anomie, rootlessness, and alienation. Communal life based on direct interpersonal communication yielded to correspondence by letter and telephone. Money became the greater determinant and measure of social relations. The impersonal transactions of the accounting book replaced the personal and informal intimacy of the local marketplace.

In the postindustrial economy, by contrast, a significant shift occurs in the labor force. A majority no longer works in agriculture or manufacturing, and the expression "the service economy" becomes almost synonymous with the new economic order. The service economy features such growing enterprises as hotels and restaurants (including the proliferating "fast food" outlets), overnight mail deliveries, sports, health clubs, entertainment and the arts, travel agencies, governmental bureaucracies, real estate, the airlines industry, education, and health care services.

Many analysts believed that postindustrial society signified above all an information society. Whereas the predecessor industrial society focused on the coordination of humans and machines, postindustrial society organized around communications and the dissemination of knowledge. Media services—newspapers, journals, radio, and especially television—increasingly provided the information that informed the daily lives of individual citizens. The electronics revolution, above all in the exploding computer industry, helped process and disseminate information with dizzying speed. Theoretical knowledge assumed greater centrality. Businesses and the military component of the federal government allocated vast expenditures for research and development, and whole divisions within a corporation dedicated themselves to product innovation and modification. The growth of the science-based industries of polymers and artificial fibers, optics, electronics, computers, aerospace, drugs, and biotechnology products marked new activities in the economy. They began to eclipse the older industries of iron and steel and their attendant products of automobiles, airplanes, and ships. In 1975, there were some six thousand research and development (R&D) laboratories in the United States.

Demographics also shaped the postindustrial society. Declining birthrates, especially among the white middle classes, became more noticeable. Increasingly, women, through modern birth control devices and through the cultural changes that would afford them greater choices for activities outside the home, opted not to have children, or they postponed having children. Many

2

delayed marriage; many more opted for divorce. (The divorce rate in 1960 was 2.2 per thousand; in 1965, 2.5; in 1970, 3.5; in 1975, 4.8; and by 1980 it had risen to 5.2 per thousand.) The very nature of the postindustrial economy affected these choices. It afforded abundant opportunities for leisure and health, for the arts, for amusements of many kinds. Its temptations were clearly tugging at traditional roles and reshaping family patterns. Indeed, the very word "lifestyle," with its connotations of choices and options, of personal discretion, gave the 1970s a linguistic turn that helped define its social and even its political culture.

The emergence of a postindustrial United States coincided with painful, sometimes traumatic effects. For one, the nation's world industrial leadership faded. American manufacturers, in such crucial activities as steel production, too long ignored the greater efficiency achieved by technological advancements in Western Europe and Japan. American producers failed to upgrade their machinery or open their corporate hierarchies to younger and more innovative managers. Compared to the competition, Americans simply no longer produced good steel. Whereas as recently as 1947 the United States produced 60 per cent of the world's steel, by 1975 it produced only 16 per cent.

The American electronics industry best symbolizes the peculiar twists of the postindustrial economy. On the one hand it tells a story of spectacular successes. For example, constant technological innovation had transformed a bulky desk-top business calculator into a hand-held device capable of highly complex mathematical computations. And it came at a fraction of the cost of its predecessor model. Americans also pioneered in the "chip" that would make the computer industry a take-off component of the economy in the 1970s and 1980s. But American manufacturers of radios and televisions had begun to establish their manufacturing and assembly operations overseas. Home construction would almost disappear by decade's end. By this time, too, the runaways included the giants of the semiconductor business: Texas Instruments, Hewlett-Packard, Intel, and others.[3]

Decline marked other American industries, most visibly the automobile. Here too, competitors gained in the market, claiming 15 percent of domestic sales in the early 1970s. With soaring inflation and accelerating fuel costs also plaguing the industry, American production fell dramatically in the middle seventies. Recalls for production and assembly defects compounded the problem as consumer confidence declined. Indeed, at the bottom of the industry's trials lay the fact of poor quality. In other industries like machine tools and high-tech electronics—televisions, radios, tape recorders—the United States conceded more and more to foreign producers.

Worse, rather than emulate or challenge the competition through innovation, these American manufacturers, too, often moved their production to Mexico, Taiwan, or South Korea. There they employed a cheaper labor force that made parts imported into the United States as semifinished materials.

The consequent loss of well-paying blue-collar jobs in the United States had extensive effects. It compelled many women to enter the American workforce simply to protect the buying power of their families. Their presence gave numerical enhancement to those enterprises associated with the rising service economy. The labor movement, in turn, now confronted a serious obstacle. During the 1970s the AFL-CIO lost more than a fourth of its membership and its once mighty political clout in Washington. The pattern elicited a postindustrial-size complaint from a union official. The United States, he said, was becoming "a nation of hamburger stands . . . a nation stripped of industrial capacity and meaningful work . . . a nation of citizens busily buying and selling cheeseburgers and root beer floats."[4] Postindustrial work seemed to lack the substantial, solid, productive quality of the industrial age.

Also, a significant demographic shift accompanied the postindustrial advent. The Midwest and Northeast sections of the country, the traditional heart of its industrial base, lost population. Simultaneously Americans moved in great numbers to the West, Southwest, and South where economic growth significantly outpaced that of the older sections. The terms *Sun Belt* and *Rust Belt* entered common discourse. These expanding areas also became the loci of the postindustrial growth and of non-union components of the changing economy. West Coast firms, beginning in California, led the information revolution. California's Silicon Valley became the great symbol of the computer revolution. It added more than a half million jobs and billions of dollars in profits to Santa Clara County in the 1970s. In the boom areas, bigger cities like Phoenix and smaller ones like Boca Raton, Florida had immense population gains, while old industrial cities like Cleveland, Buffalo, Pittsburgh, Boston, and Philadelphia lost numbers. Philadelphia, for example, lost 20 per cent of its jobs in the decade. And as David Clark has pointed out, every state in a continuous belt from Connecticut and Delaware on the East Coast and inland to Missouri experienced a decline in the number of goods produced. Lifestyle choices spurred this transition. People were losing their tolerance for the stress of cities or the cold of the "frost belt" and now opted for the sunshine of the West and South. Postindustrialism's amenities applied even to climate.

Within the metropolitan areas themselves, significant shifts occurred. The location of businesses and jobs shifted from the city to the suburbs. This shift meant a relocation of money, too, with devastating impact on the inner city. The "core" became ominously a place of unemployment, abandoned housing, racial segregation, drug abuse, and crime-ridden streets. The pathologies of America's inner-city inhabitants would be a crucial challenge among the social effects of postindustrialism.

In the 1970s, the most intriguing literature about postindustrial America focused on the changes wrought in the more comfortable quarters of white America. One could survey a copious collection of such materials, but this chapter will concentrate on three contributions to the subject. Each became a kind of cause célèbre of its own and conveyed the flavor of the postindustrial environment.

The first major book to focus on the changes to white America made its debut with the new decade itself. Twenty years later, an individual could still walk into bookstores and find the little book in bright red, green, or blue covers. It was Alvin Toffler's *Future Shock*. It ascended to the top of the best-seller lists in early 1970 and joined an emerging small literary genre of social forecasting. Publication coincided with the passing of the tumultuous sixties, and *Future Shock* marked a new mood of analysis. Forecasters like Toffler measured the national pulse not by the stormy politics of Chicago '68 or the smoking ghettoes of the inner cities; they focused on a quieter, but no less profound revolution. Toffler looked at the economic changes affecting the Western world, and the United States most emphatically. He used the descriptive label the "super industrial economy" to locate the catalyst of change in the emerging new era. The silent revolution, he said, would change institutional life from family to office, but it would alter the whole feel of people's inner existence as well.

The key fact about change in the 1970s, Toffler believed, was the very pace of it. No previous culture had lived with so fundamental a condition. Impermanence and transience in all things made orientation to the new the only constant of modern life. Toffler wanted to make a specific methodological point here. Whereas historians customarily study the past to shed light on the present, he said, it was imperative now to study the future for the same illumination. The future must become an intellectual tool. It, not the past, defines our only principle of continuity. We otherwise face the chaos of future shock, a free fall into confusion and disorientation as the temporal process outpaces our every step. In a suggestive reflection, Toffler remarked that the inhabitants of the earth are differentiated not only by race, religion, and culture, but by their experience of time. Future shock applied to the 2 or 3 percent of the human race who were people neither of the past nor of the present, but whose whole orientation to daily life was futuristic. Though small in number, "they already form an international nation of the future in our midst. They are the advance agents of man, the earliest citizens of the worldwide superindustrial nation now in the throes of birth."[5]

The superindustrial economy meant synonymously for Toffler the "second industrial revolution." His own description of the new conditions soon became a familiar one. The modern world, he observed, was passing from its industrial age. Agriculture had declined to 15 percent of the work force, and now white collar jobs outnumbered blue collar. Retail trade, administration, communications, research, and education prevailed on the economic landscape. In short, wrote Toffler, in the United States, "the world's first service economy had been born."[6]

If the postindustrial experience serves, as I hope to show it does, as a paradigm description of the intellectual and cultural history of the 1970s, then

Toffler's book provides graphic accounts of the social norms underlying that history. Culture in this decade became almost schizophrenically poised on one side or the other of the modernist continuum that Toffler described. The chapters ahead will reveal what form that dichotomy assumed, but we should note first that Toffler insisted that postindustrialism was not merely a statistical phenomenon; it had a specific "feel." "We no longer 'feel' life as men did in the past," he wrote. "And this is the ultimate difference, the distinction that separates the truly contemporary man from all others."[7] In postindustrialism, things take on greater abstraction, amorphousness, intangibility. The sense of solidness, permanence, and wholeness yields to fissures, disintegration, intangibility. What Toffler described as modes of our subjective and social experiences became, I hope to show, a pervasive leitmotif of the cultural 1970s. Some expressions of that culture reflected that quality, others valorized it for political purposes, and still others resisted it by seeking to recover history or re-experience the commonplace.

In postindustrial life, by Toffler's analysis, all relations become increasingly transient and impermanent. Relations that once endured for near lifetimes have become drastically foreshortened. Human contacts become increasingly ad hoc, defined by functions that have no greater life-span than their contractual specificity allows. Thus people live with the inescapable sense of rootlessness and discontinuity. The social bonds become ethereal, lacking staying power and unable to provide the sense of personal identification that anchors people in a substantive reality. Toffler called this experience the state of "high transience." It would be manifest in both the external and internal measures of our experiences.

Impermanence described postindustrialism's transformation of people's relation to each other, Toffler insisted, and their relation to things as well. When we think how much of all previous human experience has been defined by stable relations to a familiar environment, Toffler believed, we confront an arresting if overlooked fact of modern life. People of the ancient village used and reused tools. By contrast, modern routine defines the "throw away society":

> Diapers, bibs, paper napkins, facial tissues, towels, nonreturnable soda bottles—all are used up quickly in [the modern] home and ruthlessly eliminated. Corn muffins come in baking tins that are thrown away after one use. Spinach is encased in plastic sacks that can be dropped into a pan of boiling water for heating, and then thrown away. TV dinners are cooked and often served on throw away trays. [The home] is a large processing machine through which objects flow, entering and leaving, at a faster and faster rate of speed.[8]

If this description seems distinctly nonshocking today, let us remember that it was new enough in 1970 that Toffler could say to his readers, in effect, look, we have come to this already!

Postindustrialism produces an economics of impermanence. Advancing technology lowers the cost of manufacturing while repair work and restoration remain as an older, and expensive, category of craftsmanship. It simply becomes cheaper to replace than to repair. Historic buildings and city landmarks succumb to the economics of expediency and face the wrecking ball. Toffler called this new habit the "New York City" phenomenon, but it was almost universal in the United States.[9]

There appeared other signs of the abbreviated relations of people to things. Apartment living, or the trend toward residential renting, was changing the demographics of place. Apartment living meant shorter commitments of time to a particular place, to say nothing of the reduced sense of personal oneness with the edifice that provided one's roof. Whereas one's automobile had provided something of that sense, now the boom in rent-a-car gave a different tone to mobility. Toffler observed that among some urbanites, many of them on the go constantly and otherwise facing heavy costs for parking, car rental replaced car ownership altogether. Among those whom Toffler called the "people of the future," the "new migrants" stood out visibly. There was never previously a group of people for whom distance meant less, he said. "Never have man's relationships with place been more numerous, fragile and temporary." Whereas industrial society grew as people forsook agricultural life, postindustrial mobility derived heavily from job relocation required by technological change. The great pacesetter in high technology, International Business Machines (IBM), came to mean "I've Been Moved." Toffler added that postindustrial society represented an historic decline in the significance of place and of the tangible entities that define locale.[10]

Daniel Bell offered the most thorough analysis of the emerging new social order. His book *The Coming of Post-Industrial Society* appeared in 1973. Bell, an important thinker for the 1970s, had already established an influential intellectual career, particularly with his 1960 book *The End of Ideology*. His descriptive characteristics of postmodernism became standard in the ensuing discussions of the subject. His depiction of the social and political power arrangements in postindustrialism inspired some of the neoconservatives.

Bell began by making three basic distinctions. He described preindustrial society as one in which extractive processes dominate—agriculture, mining, fishing, lumbering, and the exploitation of fuel sources. An industrial economy is, by contrast, primarily the manufacture of goods by means of energy and machine technology. A postindustrial economy is one of processing, in which telecommunications and computers organize, disseminate, and exchange information. This postindustrial economy, Bell added, has two important features—the centrality of *theoretical* knowledge and the seminal presence of a knowledge class.[11]

Like Toffler, Bell found in the three historical eras a different "feel," different accents of life, different paces of human activity. Thus, preindustrial society pits people against nature. "One works with raw muscle power, in inherited ways, and one's sense of the world is conditioned by dependence on the elements—the seasons, the nature of the soil, the amount of water." Here the sense of time is one of *durée*, of repetition, but always with a sense of the capriciousness of things, the whim of nature.[12] In industrial societies, by contrast, life becomes rational and technical. "The machine predominates," Bell wrote, "and the rhythms of life are mechanically paced; time is chronological, methodical, evenly paced." Energy has replaced raw muscle and becomes the basis of productivity. The engineer and the semiskilled worker replace the traditional craftsman. We enter a world of scheduling and programming, a world of hierarchy and bureaucracy. The working human being becomes a part of a larger system of processes integrated efficiently into a functioning whole.[13]

Postindustrial society, too, has its own norms. "A postindustrial society," Bell wrote, "is based on services. Hence it is a game between persons. What counts is not raw muscle power, or energy, but information." The key type is the professional, equipped by education and training to provide the technical and often esoteric expertise that this society demands. But Bell found another important contrast to industrial life. "If an industrial society is defined by the quantity of goods as marking a standard of living," said Bell, "the postindustrial society is defined by the quality of life as measured by the services and amenities—health, education, recreation, and the arts—which are now deemed desirable and possible for everyone." The two characteristics both inspire and feed on each other. The postindustrial economy flourishes with restaurants, hotels, auto services, travel agents and tour packages, and entertainments, from sports to music extravaganzas. Among these amenities, education and health, whole business industries in themselves, emerge as objects of special focus, and the demands for greater access to them become political pressure points.[14]

Knowledge stood as the critical factor in postindustrialism, but knowledge of a particular kind. In postindustrial societies, Bell wrote, theory assumes a greater directive role in organizing decisions and directing exchange. Its place in social control becomes more decisive and must therefore have a more specified institutional base. Thus, as Bell observed, the great industries of the nineteenth- and early twentieth-century industrial era—steel, electric power, telegraph, telephone, automobiles, airplanes—were mainly the creation of inspired inventors and talented tinkers. They could work and succeed outside the centers of theoretical scientific inquiry. But from the new corporation to the centers of government, theory became indispensable to effective decision making and policy formulation. Bell cited the examples of econometric models of the economy that had become important for business forecasting. In many modes of its operation, postindustrial society moved along through theoretical knowledge, through the codification of knowledge into abstract systems of symbols that one could translate and apply in different circumstances. Bell even mentioned the possibility of "controlled experiments"—through systems analysis and linear programming—that could plot alternate futures for an entire nation. Finally, the primary locus of theoretical activity, the university, would be the central institution of the postindustrial era, as the business corporation had been in the industrial era.[15]

Bell's writings made him a latter-day Thorstein Veblen. His interests took him into speculations about technology and culture, and about power and politics. The progenitors of the postindustrial order, Bell believed, would necessarily be at odds with other components of their society. Like Veblen, in his discussions of the engineers, Bell with his new technocrats saw a mind-view distinctly appropriate to its functions, but thriving in a different perceptual world from the rest of society. This new technocracy, he said, accentuated logical thinking and a problem-solving, instrumental habit of mind. "It is a world view quite opposed to the traditional and customary religious, aesthetic, and intuitive modes" of thinking, he wrote. Bell posited a neo-Newtonian rationalism on the horizon and referenced thinkers from Hume to Swift to Weber. They described for him a war of the systematic mind against the prejudicial temperament that governed and sustained custom and tradition in other quarters of society. We recall, though, that Veblen had envisioned the "discipline of the machine process" making its inroads between the workers and engineers and only belatedly among the owners of capital, where the irrational ethic of business enterprise prevailed.[16]

Bell's analysis of postindustrial society gave special attention to its realignment of the power structure that attended its arrival. Here Bell was especially prescient in his forecasting. He saw a new class assuming an ascendancy in postindustrial society, a "knowledge class" that in various quarters of business and government was critically situated to exercise influence. Even the corporate centers of power, Bell observed, became dependent on the sources of knowledge information, a critical shift from the previous industrial arrangement. And if government had inherited much of business's decision-making power, Bell observed, it also took its direction from theoretical models and data input provided from the knowledge industry.[17]

One could quite properly, then, Bell believed, speak of a new elite, a new meritocracy. For one thing, more and more of postindustrial society's career tracks required specific credentialing, not through the informality of apprenticeship, but through the precise standards and content of academic programming. Within the business corporation, for example, upward mobility from shop to middle manager or beyond became a less frequent pattern of advancement. Different functions within the corporation became professionalized, using their own occult expertise and specialized training. Bell observed here another reinforcing factor in the centrality of the university in postindustrial society—its role as arbiter of class position, even of social stratification.[18]

Nevertheless, Bell described the new pattern, and the new postindustrial elite, in terms of egalitarian progress. Whereas preindustrial society had evolved into a system of estate privilege that gave honorific precedence to title

9

and nobility, land, the church, and the army, the modern society of industrialism prepared for careers open to talent. The capitalist and the entrepreneur, Bell related, replaced the landed gentry, the government administrator superseded the army, and the intelligentsia succeeded the priesthood. In the United States, however, the new locations of power remained the privilege of the WASP ethnic group. The elite universities trained the sons of that group and connected them to the hierarchies ruled by their fathers. Now that connection, too, Bell believed, had weakened. The Anglo-Saxon professoriat yielded to one increasingly Jewish, and the universities became more socially and ethnically inclusive. Bell concluded: "The postindustrial society, in this dimension of status and power, is the logical extension of the meritocracy; it is the codification of a new social order based, in principle, on the priority of educated talent."[19]

This situation, however, induced a particular irony. Greater access to power, Bell wrote, produced a new meritocracy that became a perceived center of privilege, even of a new *inequality*. In 1973, Bell could see a new democratic pressure arriving to American politics. At this time, it appeared to be mostly the inspiration of liberal and leftist attacks on the prevailing order. Demands increased for open admissions into universities, for more blacks or Hispanics, and greater representation of women in university and business positions. Affirmative action programs had begun by executive order of President Johnson in 1965. They would soon intensify in other public programs, from the state capitals to the local police and fire departments.[20]

Postindustrialism to this extent was inducing a revolution in the meaning of rights and opportunity. "What is at stake today," Bell wrote, "is the redefinition of equality." The new conditions created an unrelenting pressure for an equality of statistical parity, for the numerical correspondence of representation of groups in the power structure to their representation in the society. Bell perceived here a profound reorientation in the substance of American values. This linking of rights to membership in a particular class seemed to erode a traditional association of rights with open opportunities for individuals, without distinctions of race or sex. Bell thus commented: "What is extraordinary about this change is that, without public debate, an entirely new principle of rights has been introduced into the polity."[21]

One could even say that a double irony attended this postindustrial change. Bell had earlier observed that the conditions of postindustrialism, especially its preoccupation with "quality of life" issues, gave a considerable leverage of influence to government—education, medical care, food programs. Planning, issuing from all the locations of the public bureaucracy, assumed a greater presence in all spheres of social decision-making. Government directive would also yield to the enormous pressure to create equal access to the avenues of power and to achieve statistical parity thereby. Politics would become the arena of contending social factions and interest groups, each seeking enhancement of its privileges. But this very consequence, we shall see in later chapters, energized a populism of the right, resolved to counterattack the phenomenon of statistical equality and protesting vociferously against the "New Class" elite of the postindustrial era.

In the judgment of some writers, postindustrial society perpetrated a particular form of inner life, product of the powerful external changes that described this society. One writer in particular offered a critical diagnosis. Christopher Lasch published *The Cultural of Narcissism: American Life in an Age of Diminishing Expectations* in 1978. Lasch had written considerably on liberalism and the Left in the United States—*The American Liberals and the Russian Revolution* (1962), *The New Radicalism in America, 1889-1963* (1965), and *The Agony of the American Left* (1969)—and this work reflected his own leftist perspectives.[22]

The situation Lasch addressed derived from what he called "the political crisis of capitalism." The postindustrial phenomena he described in his book followed a particular historical destiny, "carrying the underlying principles of capitalism to their logical conclusion." This view reflected leftist assumptions about the economic future of the West (more starkly evident in Marxists' favorite reference to "late capitalism"). It also revealed in Lasch some sympathy with earlier bourgeois society—its solid moral ethic, its communalism, and its unifying cultural tradition. Now, though, Lasch could see only the ruins of these once preserving ties; all that remained was postindustrial thinness and the anarchy of individualism, the marks of modern decadence. "This book," Lasch wrote, " . . . describes a way of life that is dying—the culture of competitive individualism, which in its decadence has carried the logic of individualism to the extreme of a war of all against all, the pursuit of happiness to the dead end of a narcissistic preoccupation with the self."[23] *The Culture of Narcissism* often registered the anger of a political leftist and the lament of a cultural conservative.

Much in Lasch's survey reinforced what became in the 1970s a normative descriptive literature of postindustrial conditions. But in Lasch it had particular pungency. We seemed to live, he wrote, within an existential collapse of time. Our historical senses were vague; the past could not inform or direct our understanding. Instead, we had only nostalgia, a past built of symbol and sentiment, and readily exploited as marketable commodity. Bourgeois values, on the other hand, had so eroded (an inflationary economy abetted the cultural shift) that we lived without a sense of the future as well. Indefinite hedonism thus came to dominate the modern psyche. "Restless, perpetually unsatisfied desire" moved mass society on its rudderless course. Indefinite purpose, or what one could best describe as an indiscriminate success ethic, defined our competitive business activity. So insubstantial had become the self of the contemporary individual, so poorly rooted in meaningful experience, so attenuated with respect to any concrete tradition or intimate sense of time, that even its wants had to be defined by advertising or the many service-priests of a therapeutic culture.[24]

To Lasch, postindustrial culture was emphatically therapeutic. After the political turmoil of the 1960s Americans retreated headlong to the "purely personal," he wrote. Loss of hope in redeeming the world outside promoted a turn to inner psychic self-improvement. From health food to Eastern religion, or to any pursuit that brought people in touch with their "feelings," therapeutic culture redefined the sense of reality and intensified historical discontinuity. Lasch took care to point out that this turn inward bore little correspondence with the introspection that marked the authentic religious experience that described some previous ages. "The contemporary climate is therapeutic," he wrote, "not religious. People today hunger not for personal salvation . . . but for the feeling, the momentary illusion, of personal well-being, health, and psychic security."[25]

For Lasch, therapeutic culture could not bear the burden of social improvement. He drew this painful conclusion by observing that the political Left itself had been primal victim of the consciousness ideology. This historian of the American Left now saw the Left as the very victim of the society it wished so badly to reconstruct. In the odyssey of ex-radical Jerry Rubin (one of the infamous "Chicago Seven" in the 1960s), that is, in what Rubin called his "journey into myself," Lasch discerned the fatuous politics of inner reconstruction. Rubin's battles against his own inner demons, Lasch said, deprived his radicalism of the needed social insights. Lasch believed that the New Left once promised a useful link between politics and culture, between subjective experience and objective social reconstruction. But the alliance of the sixties became sundered in the seventies. The Left, so far as Rubin represented it, Lasch believed, had abandoned the political arena and lapsed into liberationist clichés.[26]

The Culture of Narcissism made a powerful contribution to the literature of postindustrialism because it so persuasively chronicled the thinness and insubstantiality that described its culture. Thus, Lasch carefully distinguished the American individualism of the nineteenth century, captured by Tocqueville's summations, and exemplified by Emerson and others who constructed the "American Adam" as national prototype. Lasch sympathized with the critics of that representative individualism—Orestes Brownson, Henry James, Van Wyck Brooks—but, as much in regret as in pique, he described seventies individualism—therapeutic individualism—as essentially spurious. The latter individualism, he said, thrives only because ego and personality have been thoroughly deflated by the forces of political domination and by the entire socialization process. "In our time," Lasch wrote, "this invasion of private life by the forces of organized domination has become so pervasive that personal life has almost ceased to exist." Human selfhood, Lasch believed, had lost its resistive power, its own integral identity. Increasingly it took on the dominant qualities of late capitalism, its anarchic individualism, its combativeness, its coarseness.[27]

Lasch's many reflections on the modern situation yielded a particular impression of postindustrial life. The dominant trait was its inauthenticity.

But Lasch worried less about "false consciousness" than about the structures and experiences of interpersonal relations and with the imposing difficulty of joining our consciousness to tangible reality. He wrote:

> We live in a swirl of images and echoes that arrest experience and play it back in slow motion. Cameras and recording machines not only transcribe experience but alter its quality, giving to much of modern life the character of an enormous echo chamber, a hall of mirrors. Life presents itself as a succession of images or electronic signals, of impressions recorded and reproduced by means of photography, motion pictures, televisions, and sophisticated recording devices. Modern life is so thoroughly mediated by electronic images that we cannot help responding to others as if our actions—and their own—were being recorded and simultaneously transmitted to an unseen audience or stored up for close scrutiny at a later time.[28]

These effects, Lasch believed, helped redefine corporate life, too. Like Toffler, he perceived a decline of the proverbial "organization man," but he supplied a different account. Business success, he believed, did not any longer derive from loyalty to a concrete institution, to a cognizable pattern of company mores and familial ways. The manipulation of interpersonal relations counted most; meaningful personal relations less. Performance counted for less than "visibility," and result less than "momentum." The narcissistic businessman flourishes not in a world of concrete problem-solving, but in a milieu of personal impressions that he manages skillfully.[29]

In a society where all relations became increasingly amorphous, Lasch observed, the new corporate life found replication in other quarters. Politics became the manipulation of information, as the great political drama of the 1970s, Watergate, illustrated. Crisis management and spin control, the play of events before the media, mattered more than concrete issues themselves.[30] At another level, sexual relations, too, succumb to postindustrial inauthenticity. In what he called "the flight from feeling," Lasch described changing social and cultural patterns that documented the fear of intimacy and the premium of emotional disengagement. The new ideology of sexual liberation, Lasch observed, sought to remove from personal relations their primal passions— jealousy, possessiveness, commitment—that is, all the emotional risk that genuine intimacy must bring.[31]

The analysts of postindustrialism orient us to 1970s cultural and intellectual life. Postindustrial consciousness thrives with a feeling of unreality about all things, of a loss of substance, immediacy, tangibility, and wholeness. As such, it underscores the whole cultural effect of postmodernism. Symbol becomes more significant than fact, appearance more than reality; image becomes essence, theory transcends analysis. In academic discourse one hears much about the death of the subject, the decentered self, the dissolution of meaning, the pluralistic and invisible character of power, and the absent cause. 1970s intellectual history found its special qualities as it negotiated its way through the gaps and fissures of postindustrial modernity, finding new opportunities but also making repairs.

two

Wars of Words

Literary theory provided a key focus for the cultural politics of the 1970s. The subject became a contested ground, one in which the French presence in particular gave it an international setting and a cosmopolitan air. Even undergraduates at American colleges and universities found themselves mastering a new vocabulary. "Structuralism," "poststructuralism," and "deconstruction" signaled the new modes of understanding and interpretation. Others like "semiotics," "diachronic," "aporia," and "binary oppositions" gave resplendence, if not esoterica, to the academic discourse of the classroom and the examination booklets.

Many found literary theory an intimidating enterprise. Its practitioners flaunted technical and forbidding scholarly prose. To some, its work exemplified the isolation and obscurantism that were depriving higher education of its humanistic calling and contribution to public discussion. The war of the word, many felt, signified only a war of words.

For at least three reasons, however, a selective survey of the intellectual life of the 1970s profits from an examination of these conflicts. For one, they enriched the intellectual scene in the United States by influences from abroad. Names like Lévi-Strauss, Barthes, Foucault, Habermas, Derrida, and Lacan influenced new strategies of interpretation in several academic disciplines. They thus also had a synthesizing effect, cutting across old and hardened boundaries. Structuralism in anthropology, for example, suggested new approaches to the study of literature. Reading texts offered clues to reading society and to deciphering the power arrangements in it. The new literary theory also suggests the "feel" of postindustrial society as visited in the preceding chapter. We enter a domain where tangibility loosens, where the center evaporates, where an overwhelming multiplicity of signs and encodings fractures wholeness and unity. Infinite regress erodes the sense of presence.

Second, literature, and really literary criticism in particular, became the focal point of long and varied trends that realized their culminating effects in the 1970s. As the political program of the Left self-destructed in the early part of the decade, the leftist agenda assumed a greater focus on culture. It moved to the universities. It rediscovered neo-Marxist, or "Western" Marxist formulations that had long been influential on the other side of the Atlantic. The adaptation and extension of these influences in the United States made the 1970s a significant chapter in the intellectual history of the American Left. Did the intellectual Left in the process gain new measures of sophistication and useful means of political reform? Or was its cultural program a lapse into the recondite and irrelevant cocoon of academia, a measure of its defeat in the political and economic arena? Some thinkers on the Left (curiously allied with academic traditionalists) decried the new directions: endless reams of scholarship, the turgid MLA programs, the intellectual minutia. Word games.

Third, these literary matters raised anew, and in fresh ways, old questions about Western civilization. They forced debate about the social role of the humanities, and about class and culture. They recharged ancient philosophical questions about knowledge, the self, and the meaning of truth. The political Left as noted, especially, had a stake in these issues. Literature, and culture in all its aspects, it insisted, partook of every ploy and every social nuance of capitalist society. Art and the aesthetic domain would, under Marxist reformulation, be hard pressed to gain for themselves any independence from their social milieu. They were joined to the enduring class structures of industrial capitalism and its postindustrial complex. They were understood, in Marxist description, as an inseparable part of the comprehensive processes of production, domination, and the money nexus. For all their technical language, the debates that raged in American literary criticism reflected important political issues in areas seemingly beyond its habitat. In the process they gave the humanities a larger field of work and prompted engaging intramural warfare.

In 1916 there appeared a book called *Course de Linguistique Générale*, the posthumous work of a Swiss scholar. He had taught at the Ecole des Hautes Etudes in Paris, and had died three years previously. Some of his students reconstructed notes from their professor's lectures and with the resultant book, twentieth-century linguistics was born.

Ferdinand de Saussure had some intriguing things to say about language. He distinguished the use of particular words by individuals (*paroles*) from systematic, structured languages (*langues*), such as French and German, that existed at a given time in a given society. He also distinguished synchronic language, as it exists at a given time, from its diachronic patterns, which change over time. In other ways, too, Saussure used terminology that has governed much of modern linguistic theory. He designated "sign" (a written word) as an entity that unites "signifier" (the sound of the word) and the "signified" (the concept or thing). But words, of course, do not derive their meaning from any inherent character of their sound. To convey sense, said Saussure, a word has to assume meaning in comparison with another word. This differentiation makes language precisely what it is—a pattern, or code, of differences that converts arbitrarily selected sounds into usable communication. Saussure also informs us that what is significant in language is what is left out. Such a notion would carry potential radical political implications. Saussure furthermore explained that words do not serve as precise correlates or representations of the world outside. The order and structure of that world are determined for us by our language. Saussure, in effect, restricted our sense of reality to the inner forms shaped by language. What is signified is not an object of knowledge that enters our thought as a presentation, but a concept that is the form in which we experience some outer realm of being. Saussure could also say, then, that language is the determinant, the structure of our thought. He wrote in the *Course* that "in itself, thought is like a swirling cloud, where no shape is intrinsically determinate . . . and nothing is distinct before the introduction of linguistic structure."[1]

Saussure's ideas were becoming known in the United States in the early 1970s. But more dramatic for the American audience was the intellectual achievement of Claude Lévi-Strauss, the French structuralist. Lévi-Strauss's massive scholarship included his *Elementary Structures of Kinship* (1949), his four-volume *Mythologiques* (1964-1971), and *The Savage Mind* (1966). Lévi-Strauss undertook an investigation of more than eight hundred North and South American Indian myths, with the ultimate conclusion that all of them may be variants of a single one. Myths, for Lévi-Strauss, became a kind of language, with their own rules of grammar that constituted the myths' true "meaning." "Whatever our ignorance of the language and the culture of the people where it originated," wrote Lévi-Strauss, "a myth is still felt as a myth by any reader anywhere in the world."[2]

Myths, then, revealed for Lévi-Strauss not so much a narrative content, but forms that disclose to us the constructs of the human mind. Moreover, these mental operations become the means by which the mind organizes experience. Lévi-Strauss thus stands in the tradition of Kantian epistemology. (Philosopher Paul Ricoeur more appropriately called Lévi-Strauss's formulation "a Kantism without a transcendental subject.") Mythology was not significant for the narrative stories spun from a thinking subject because, said Lévi-Strauss, myths think themselves through people. Here Lévi-Strauss expressed an important theme in modern literary considerations—the notion of the decentered subject. "One result of structuralism," it has been said, "is the 'decentering' of the individual subject, who is no longer to be regarded as the source or end of meaning." Lévi-Strauss' work, like Saussure's, constituted a synchronic formulation that denies primacy both to historical situation and individual presence. In the judgment of one uneasy historian, we are left with a "monolithic determinism" that dissolves the individual subject, a notion essential to traditional humanistic understanding.[3]

The reception of structuralism brought attending shock waves. Its approaches to literature challenged some of the most ingrained assumptions of the ordinary reader or student of literature. In the 1970s, one began to hear that the author is "dead"; that literature really writes itself; that writers cannot use language to express themselves, only to draw upon a vast compendium of signs for a literature that "is always already written." These ideas gained attention in America through the translated writings of French theorist Roland Barthes. His early works, especially *Mythologies* (1957; American publication, 1977) and his *Elements of Semiology* (1968) held a particular fascination in the United States. Barthes wrote, in a summary statement of his structuralist period, that "man does not exist prior to language."[4] Language structured identity and did so monolithically.

Structuralism had political implications. It dominated the intellectual life of France in the 1960s and won the allegiance of the Left in particular. Indeed, structuralism has been described as an attempt to transpose Marxism into a new epistemological context. It moves Marxism beyond its idealistic roots in Hegel and its own economic determinism into a different kind of scientific system.[5] Marxists perceived strategical advantages in structuralism. It subjected human culture to a system of controlling laws. Within this system such "bourgeois" notions of the individual subject, the independent "self" that is the location of meaning and knowledge, lost their ontologically privileged status. It further discredited such high humanistic notions of an order of reality "out there," a fixed order of things in which were embodied higher truths that language could reflect. Structuralism, as some Marxists welcomed it, threatened the ideological security of those who would wish the world to be within their control through language that mirrored timeless intellectual truths.[6]

But in another sense, that was precisely the problem. For in the end, the intellectual Left found itself distinctly uncomfortable with structuralism. The Marxists in particular perceived in structuralism a kind of philosophical idealism that rendered concrete history irrelevant to the understanding of culture. It deprived history of those factors of class and economics that made Marxism not only a materialistic understanding of human life, but a dynamic, dialectical process. Here the contending issues of "synchronic" and "diachronic" modes of understanding came into play. Marxism looked to the historical changes and conflicts in society, while structuralism retreated to the mental constructs that language reveals, constructs embedded in a universal mind that transcended any particular culture. The American Marxist Fredric Jameson charged that structuralism left us trapped in the "prison-house of language." Earlier the French existentialist-turned-Marxist, Jean-Paul Sartre, called structuralism a "trick of the bourgeoisie, an attempt to substitute for the Marxist vision of evolution a closed inert system where order is privileged at the expense of change."[7] In the United States, books by Robert Scholes[8] and Jonathan Culler suggested the acceptance of a structuralist literary philosophy. The versatile Culler would be a conduit to this country of many of the French currents. He urged in his *Structuralist Poetics* that theory served to provide a legitimating framework for insights that a "competent" reader might discern and that might otherwise elude detection. Structuralism could provide access to texts whose "meaning" might otherwise depend on the subjective peculiarities of the individual reader. Culler's program impressed some as structuralism at its most conservative. They believed it gave credence to traditional ideas of texts as bearers of stable meanings and confirmed an older notion of the critic as a faithful seeker after truth.[9]

In the United States, Hayden White's book of 1973, *Metahistory*, made a formidable illustration of structuralism as applied to intellectual history. White focused on the great historians and philosophers of history in the nineteenth century—Jules Michelet, Leopold von Ranke, Jacob Burckhardt, Karl Marx, Friedrich Nietzsche, and others. White wanted to interrogate the processes of historical writing. In doing so he made an important shift from the primacy of the external reality, or the data base of historical fact, to the interior processes that transform that data. This effort took White, as he said at the outset of his study, to the "deep structures of the historical imagination." Those structuring activities, White argued, signified various linguistic devices, strategies the historian uses to arrange the content material of historical works. White could therefore assert that history was essentially "a poetic act" that prefigures the historical field.[10]

In all of the individuals that White studied he sought to illuminate the "structural components" of their writings. The linguistic focus of these analyses led White to examine the use by his subjects of such literary devices as metaphor, metonymy, synecdoche, and irony—the "tropological strategies" that each employed. White's skillful readings made his several chapters a series of textual readings, emphatically formalist in nature. They virtually removed the works from their own historical contexts. Indeed in White's treatment, language overrode social context as "thought remains the captive of the linguistic mode" in which it apprehends its materials. This important shift threw the business of history into epistemological doubt. For historical works, White asserted, cannot claim their veracity through the "data" they present. They gain suasion instead by "the consistency, coherence, and illuminative power of their respective visions of the historical field." For White, the best grounds for choosing one historical perspective over another are ultimately aesthetic and moral grounds more than intellectual, a qualification he repeated specifically in discussing Marx.[11]

The literary shift executed by White owed much to continental thinkers. White acknowledged Martin Heidegger, Lévi-Strauss, and Barthes, but also Michel Foucault and Jacques Derrida, associated with poststructuralism. But poststructuralism came to the United States quickly on the heels of structuralism, even as the word "structuralism" remained in use as a normative reference. White sensed Foucault's and Derrida's challenge to structuralism. He believed, however, that they, too, were captives of their own governing linguistic strategies, like the nineteenth-century historians that White studied.[12]

Structuralism had barely begun its entry into the United States when its familial next-of-kin, poststructuralism, challenged it. Poststructuralism attempted to deflate the scientific pretensions of structuralism. It did not sit easily with the orderly forms by which structuralism arranged the world. Poststructuralism brings us into an infinite diversity of experience, a free fall into indeterminacy of meaning and form. It reveled in differentiation and invited readers to take the pleasure of the text. It exempted them from obligations to honor ideas of truth. Radical poststructuralism thrived within a mood of skepticism and iconoclasm. It left the logocentric civilization of the West a shattered ruin. When the poststructuralists had done their work, what was there left to be said in literature for authorial intention? for the autonomous subject? for the collective readership? for representation? for meaning in any locale? Now it would be *sauve qui peut*.

Saussurean structuralism, as noted, posited an inseverable tie between the signifier and the signified, the constituents of the sign. But in the progress of linguistic formulations in the late 1960s that bond began to weaken. For it was now understood that meaning can have no such stationary locus. The "signified" as a Saussurean concept could no longer support itself and the signified inevitably becomes another "signifier." Meaning becomes an endlessly unwinding ball of yarn. Look up the meaning of a signifier in the dictionary and all you have before you are more signifiers. The dictionary, in short, conveys only the indefinite postponement of meaning. Poststructuralists were now saying that we glimpse meaning only in what the sign is not, that is, in the entire long chain that alone is the totality of meaning. We sense meaning as we glimpse a flickering light on a distant boat set on the ocean's horizon. It is a light that points back to us and into the unseeable beyond.[13] As Terry Eagleton put it: "The implication of all this is that language is a much less stable affair than the classical structuralists had considered. Instead of being a well-defined, clearly demarcated structure containing symmetrical units of signifiers and signified, it now begins to look much more like a sprawling limitless web where there is a constant interchange and circulation of elements, where none of the elements is absolutely definable and where everything is caught up and traced through by everything else."[14]

Language, in short, now appears to be a much less structured affair than the classical structuralists had made it. The poststructuralists quickly exploited the gap that now opened up in the Saussurean construct. Into that gap fell many sacred notions of truth, logic, language, and literature. Into this black hole of literary space, texts followed their own path to self-destruction. They became tripped up by their own ruling systems of logic. They came to an impasse, an *aporia* of meaning, came "unstuck." The process that demonstrated this inevitable procedure became known by the name of "deconstruction."[15]

Poststructuralism gained an American audience through the later trans-lated works of Barthes, especially *S/Z* (English translation, 1974). But it was the formidable Jacques Derrida who carried poststructuralism to its extremes of skepticism. Derrida was the terror of the critical establishment, drawing from Nietzsche, Edmund Husserl, Heidegger, and Saussure to make his own radical conclusions in literature and philosophy. His writings on these sub-jects were themselves unorthodox in their presentations, as they were ambiguous and enigmatic, a challenge and intimidation to many readers. As with the later Barthes, no clear division in Derrida demarcated criticism and creativity. And in the fertile mind of Derrida there was much of the latter.

From structuralism to poststructuralism, the more the study of language advanced, the more there prevailed the conviction that language is all we can ultimately know, and that most uncertainly. Derrida is therefore the quintes-sential poststructuralist. The structural forms that in Saussure and in Lévi-Strauss at least preserved an idealistic world of meaning and order now in Derrida's rendering lost their footing altogether. Language found a reference only in itself; it could not reach out to any immediate presence of being. Lan-guage was always making an infinite regress from itself, spinning an endless chain of signifiers. In Derrida, every linguistic word defined itself only by what it was not. Each element contained a "trace" of what is absent, as if it were a note in a symphony, meaningful only when experienced as part of the whole composition. Meaning always had this fluid and inconstant character. The very act of containing it constricted its fullest apprehension.

One writer summarized Derrida's analysis of literature this way:

> Derrida's dominant idea concerning the literary text is that, since language is a chain of signifiers that does not point to independently existing signi-fieds, texts do not portray a real world that exists independent of language. Consequently, criticism is to focus on the text as a construct of language, a rhetorical fabrication that can be understood by being dismantled, decon-structed to reveal its often covert rhetorical machinery. This procedure leads not to truth but rather—the benchmark of skepticism—to the under-standing that where truth was thought to be there is only an absence of truth, its perpetual evasiveness, a vacancy, an empty place, which language has masked to create the effect of completeness and unity.[16]

Derrida denied any mimetic function to writing and his cogent maxim "there is nothing outside the text" perhaps too conveniently summarized deconstructionist epistemology. But Derridean poststructuralism means that everything is a text because all things must be decoded and interpreted. Der-rida's followers would take up the challenge to read political and social sys-tems as texts.[17]

Derrida recognized that we cannot get along without "the center," without a location of authority. From there, however, his views about language departed from the basic suppositions of Western philosophy up to that time, particularly its metaphysical tradition. That tradition, logocentric to the core, had always used language to locate some principle of centrality, some basis of authority, some element of unity—in essence, some "transcendental signifier"—that would define meaning and purpose for existence. Western discourse variously centers in such concepts as the "Idea," the "Absolute," "God," the "World Spirit," "noumena," "substance," "matter." Our intellectual vocabulary is full of notional purities: "ends," "origins," "essences," "processes," "intentions."

The French imprint gained another important American application with Edward Said's book of 1975, *Beginnings: Intention and Method*. Said, born to a Palestinian family in Jerusalem in 1935, came to the United States as a refugee in 1947. He received his doctorate from Harvard in 1963 and began a teaching career at Columbia. *Beginnings* offered an often turgid analysis of a primal Western concept that Said wanted to place under scrutiny. His survey took him into extensive historical analyses of literary works, but intellectually it made open acknowledgement of French theory. Indeed, *Beginnings* introduced poststructuralism to American readers, though it was called by its predecessor's name.

To one particular intellectual Said stood in debt—Michel Foucault. Foucault was a true genius. In a most productive, but short career, Foucault left a body of writings that studied untraditional subjects and offered unorthodox conclusions. He presented no Foucauldian system as such, only an intellect that dismantled all conventional wisdom and all systems wherever he found them. Some labeled Foucault a structuralist, a label he rightly resisted, for if anything Foucault perfected the mental habits of poststructuralism. Foucault's influence increased in the United States during the 1970s from English translations of his works: *Historie de la folie* (1961) as *Madness and Civilization* in 1971; *Les mots et les choses* (1966) as *The Order of Things* in 1970. Other works followed, concluding with the uncompleted *History of Sexuality* after Foucault's death in 1982.

Said highlighted in Foucault his radical textualism, his focus on the primacy of language and sign as the realities in which we live. "The drama of Foucault's work," wrote Said, "is that he is always coming to terms with language as both the constructing horizon and the energizing atmosphere within and by which all human activity must be understood."[18] But Foucault found that in the modern era (beginning in the nineteenth century) a kind of ontological discontinuity emerges. As one illustration, the signifying power of language overwhelms what is being signified, and this because, as Said reported, "the discourse of modern knowledge always hungers for what it cannot fully grasp or totally represent." Knowledge always desperately pursues its elusive subject, inflating and overloading our logocentric experience and bringing it to its ultimate impasse.[19]

Consider the notion of "man," and its foundational status in Western humanism. This idea, Said observed, supplied to humanism an essential subject, a stable location that persists amid the flux of experience, a point of resistance, an abiding reference. Said read Foucault and perceived immediately how this notion had become dissolved, and with it the whole apparatus of Western culture.

> For if tradition and education train us to take man as the concrete universal, the pivot and the center of awareness, then Foucault makes us lose our grip on man. If we are inclined to think of man as an entity resisting the flux of experience, then because of Foucault and what he says of linguistics, ethnology, and psychoanalysis, man is dissolved in the overarching waves, the quanta, in the striations of language itself, turning finally into little more than a constituted subject, a speaking pronoun, fixed indecisively in the eternal, ongoing rush of discourse.[20]

Said recognized, too, the revolutionary consequences of this loss of the subject—a point that united Foucault, Lévi-Strauss, Barthes, and Jacques Lacan. For the idea of the thinking subject underscores normative Western notions of originality and individualism. This loss also unsettles related ideas of cause and intention, continuity, history and progress. These organizing concepts Western thinkers have projected onto the disparate chronological pieces of an experienced past. Or, as Said wrote: "History in the main has acquired its intelligibility through a kind of anthropomorphism projected onto and into events and collectivities of various sorts."[21] Our knowledge ultimately is constitutive of nothing. We can refer it neither to a privileged origin nor a telos, and with their dissolution we lose what our culture has always made the guarantors of meaning.[22] Said followed Foucault to land in radical discontinuity, accident, and decenteredness.

Decenteredness also figured prominently in the postmodernist anthropology of Clifford Geertz. A major theoretical voice in this academic discipline, Geertz also made broad contributions through his ethnographic accounts of politics, religion, economics, and ecology. These studies had taken him to Java, Bali, and Morocco. Born in San Francisco in 1923, Geertz had studied at Antioch College, Princeton, and Harvard and taught at the University of Chicago. Then he removed to the Institute for Advanced Studies at Princeton, New Jersey. Geertz had no anthropological training as an undergraduate. Instead, his contributions owed much to American philosophical pragmatism pursued in his studies at Antioch.[23]

Geertz made his major contribution in his 1973 book, *The Interpretation of Cultures*. Here he addressed some issues that had animated anthropological discussions for some time. He observed that anthropology had moved away from the Enlightenment notion of a universal human nature. It had turned to culture, and its infinite varieties, to loosen the grip of so overwhelming and controlling a concept. Instead of the expectation that one might locate "Man" as a reality "behind," "above," "under," or "beyond" the customs that describe him, the new quest assumed it possible to locate an uncapitalized "man" "in" those customs. Geertz observed that the various efforts of this kind employed an intellectual strategy that he labeled the "stratigraphic" conception of man and his associations—biological, psychological, social, and cultural. The strategy led its practitioners, Geertz described, to "peel off" each layer to expose the next. But these efforts, Geertz charged, had not liberated anthropology from its universalist Enlightenment roots. The idea of normative humanity persisted. Geertz wrote: "At the level of concrete research and specific analysis, this grand strategy came down, first, to a hunt for universals in culture, for empirical uniformities that, in the face of the diversity of customs around the world and over time, could be found everywhere in about the same form, and, second, to an effort to relate such universals, once found, to the established constants of human biology, psychology, and social organization."[24] Geertz called this program the *consensus gentium* approach and he labeled it a failure.

Geertz, to be sure, did not wish to abandon altogether the idea of "what it is to be generically human." He did believe, though, that the cultural particularities of people supply better clues to that idea than their commonalities. For Geertz found it intriguing that each human begins life with the capacity to live in a multitude of ways but in the end lives only one way. Here he employed parallel poststructuralist terminology with the suggestion that something is significant by virtue of what it is not. He further borrowed language from American pragmatic thinkers—Charles Sanders Peirce, George Herbert Mead, and John Dewey—in saying that an individual orients himself to the world by trafficking in significant symbols. These symbols embrace an expansive category of things—words, to be sure, but also gestures, drawings, tools, clothing, jewelry. We call the accumulated totality of such symbols "culture."[25]

This activity, to Geertz, signified so essential a behavior for human beings that we must define it as the very essence of human nature. Culture is not an addition to the completed human animal, but defines that animal from the first time in which it becomes recognizable as such. From the time humans submit to a system of significant symbols that system attains increasing dominance in subsequent eras. Language, myth, ritual, and social structure create the environments to which we must submit or within which we must operate to have any prospect for change. From this understanding, said Geertz, we draw one emphatic conclusion. "Most bluntly, it suggests that there is no such thing as a human nature independent of culture." Should we seek some underlying, unchanging, normative type, Geertz insisted, "we are in quest of a metaphysical entity." For the overriding and essentialist "Man" we substitute the decentered, empirical entity "man."[26]

Geertz gained attention in another way. If we are to understand human behavior in terms of the dominant significant symbols of any social system, he said, then anthropology becomes a form of textual analysis. Concerning the role of cockfighting in Bali society, for example, Geertz stressed that at issue is not a matter of social mechanics but of social semantics. "For the anthropologist, whose concern is with formulating sociological principles, not with promoting or appreciating cockfights, the question is, what does one learn about such principles from examining culture as an assemblage of texts?" Anthropology, therefore, Geertz believed, should extend the notion of text beyond written material to nonliterary and nonverbal forms.[27]

Geertz stood sufficiently in the American pragmatic tradition that his textual or "hermeneutical" anthropology also preserved an empirical basis and referenced a real world of human activity. Negotiating the dominant cultural symbols always signified for him the survival function of human intelligence. In *The Interpretation of Cultures*, which has a striking and essentially appreciative essay on Lévi-Strauss, Geertz nonetheless clearly distinguished his poststructuralist theory from the Frenchman's structuralism. Lévi-Strauss, Geertz pointed out, did not seek to understand symbolic forms in terms of how they functioned in concrete situations, that is, in organizing emotions and forming values. He sought instead to understand them strictly in terms of their internal structure, independent of all social context. That effort, Geertz said, returned anthropology to its errant Enlightenment roots. For Lévi-Strauss, the mind of man is, at bottom, everywhere the same.[28]

Geertz's prominence in this reorientation of anthropology naturally induced dissent in his discipline. In the 1960s some "materialist" anthropologists, at Columbia especially, stressed political economy. This mildly Marxist group had an interest in cultural analysis to the extent that these "surface phenomena" helped reveal underlying mechanisms of power and control within the prevailing class arrangements.[29] To these observers Geertzian textualism missed the larger point.

For example, Marvin Harris, professor at the University of Florida, associated Geertz with Derrida, Foucault, and Paul de Man, and believed he had influenced followers whose work Harris judged to be antiscientific in spirit. Geertz and company, Harris claimed, deprived anthropology of its concern with objective analysis and its standards of experiment, verification, and truth. An apologist of "cultural materialism" in anthropology, Harris resented the "elitist, obscurantist, and nihilist posturing" of postmodernist anthropology and believed it availed little in what ought to be the profession's main concerns—a political opposition to consumerism and capitalism, the threat of global corporations, the problems of social class, and the challenge of peace.[30] We can assume that Geertz did not gain any intellectual suasion with Harris when he referred to himself as "by general persuasion," a "postmodernist bourgeois liberal."[31]

Deconstruction became a major academic issue in the 1970s and by the middle of the 1980s had entered public discussion also. Writing in 1975, Yale professor J. Hillis Miller referred to the "naturalization of recent continental criticism" in the United States. He added that "literary criticism at this moment is an international enterprise." He had plenty of evidence for his statement. Acknowledging that many good, recent works in American literary scholarship had not incorporated the new perspectives, he yet believed that the tide was clearly turning. Miller mentioned new literary journals that were exploring the theories from abroad—*Diacritics, Critical Inquiry, MLN, The Georgia Review, New Literary History, Yale French Studies*. He cited a flood of new translations of the popular works of Roland Barthes and of Derrida's *Glas* in the previous year. He listed new academic strongholds of poststructuralism—Yale, SUNY Buffalo, Johns Hopkins, Cornell, Iowa. Miller could well describe these events. He was a major player in the "Yale School" of scholars who formed the vanguard of the new directions in American literary scholarship.[32]

The Yale group of Miller, Paul de Man, Geoffrey Hartman, and Harold Bloom, constituted a highly diverse, deeply learned, and complex constellation of scholars. But they effected, as it were, an "American" translation of the French methodologies and literary philosophies. It was on their readings that the American literary wars of the 1970s were joined. Deconstructionists, Marxists, and traditional humanists partook of the combat. The contest proved how quickly matters of seemingly recondite academic disputations took on large social and political dimensions.

A literature conference held at the Johns Hopkins University in 1966 signaled the French arrival to the United States. Derrida and others presented outlines of their ideas and won immediate acclaim. Publication of the conference papers and the gradual assimilating of the new language theories in American institutions would provide them the kind of visibility Miller described in 1975.

Americans did not adopt the French methods wholesale. Instead, they blended older American habits with the new ways. Thus, they validated the aesthetic as such and resisted the merging of the art product with any larger milieu, whether the personal or the social. The New Criticism, influential from the late 1930s through the 1950s, had reasserted this bias. Some would come to believe that the Yale School reestablished it on a new footing. Equally prejudicial was an American honoring of the individual subject, the autonomous creator, the self. The subjective in art, moreover, had reinforcement recently in American critical theory by other continental imports—existentialism and phenomenology in particular. Individualist and formalist notions of art proved highly tenacious.[33]

The career of J. Hillis Miller affords the most useful way of measuring the changes in question. Born in Newport News, Virginia in 1928, the son of a Baptist minister, Miller studied with Douglas Bush at Harvard University and received his Ph.D. in 1952. His academic shifts corresponded roughly with his own changing theoretical writings—Harvard (New Criticism), Johns Hopkins (phenomenology), and Yale (poststructuralism).

The Johns Hopkins years, 1953 to 1972, set an important background. A significant collegial influence on Miller was Georges Poulet, a major voice of the Geneva School of criticism, often called "phenomenological," though Poulet spurned that label. For the Geneva scholars, the study of literature meant the study of consciousness. The critic treats the entire work of an author as so many manifestations of the same authorial subject, an individual. As Poulet wrote, the critic must succeed "in refeeling, in rethinking, in re-imagining the author's thought from the inside." And as Miller would write in a famous essay on the Geneva School, the critic's "genius" lies in the "inner plasticity" that enables him "to duplicate within himself the affective quality of the mind of each of his authors." Of course, the author one comes to know is made available through texts, through language; hence, one may ask if the author can be anything other than his own language, a question that antici-pates Miller's later turn to poststructuralism.[34]

In 1958 Miller published *Charles Dickens: The World of His Novels,* dedicated to Poulet. Miller made the focus of this work the mind of the author Dickens. Through the variety of his individual works, Miller wrote, "the critic can hope to glimpse the original unity of a creative mind." For Miller it was axiomatic that all the works reflect a unity, "an implacable organizing form, constantly presiding over the choice of words."[35] Clearly, in 1958 Miller was at least a few removes from poststructuralism.

As indeed he was in his next book, *The Disappearance of God: Five Nineteenth-Century Writers* (1963). Miller studied five Victorians for whom the loss of God in modern culture is replaced by new symbols. These "late romantics," as Miller described them, honor the artist "as creator or discoverer of hitherto unappreciated symbols, symbols which establish a new relation, across the gap, between man and God."[36] But here again Miller treated the corpus of writings of each individual as a unity, and again his criticism functioned as a study of consciousness and its textual locations. Here and in *Poets of Reality* (1965), Miller chose to occupy a logocentric universe of canonical master-works.

A logocentric critical orientation notwithstanding, those two books already contained hints of the new direction Miller was to take. *The Disappearance of God* posed for Miller certain problems of language. For the very absence of God becomes the problem of ascertaining certainty in textual analysis, the problem, as Berman observes, of "the perpetual withdrawal of truth from lan-guage." Miller had arrived at this kind of abyss before the appearance of Der-rida and the poststructuralists. And with their arrival the old house of logo-centric certitude collapsed.[37]

The American opening to the French became apparent in 1972. In one of the most useful documents for our attempt to understand the American accommodation, Miller offered that year his review of M. H. Abrams' book *Natural Supernaturalism.* Miller correctly described this book, appreciatively, as a contribution in "the grand tradition of modern humanistic scholarship."[38] *Natural Supernaturalism* brilliantly interpreted the romantic literary movement as a secularization and internalization of the Judaeo-Christian view of life—a model that romanticism inherited, partly refashioned, but could not discard. Abrams described the romantics as living out the drama of grace and redemption, recovery and renewal, the quest for a new heaven and a new earth. They undertook to give new and personal meaning to these Christian categories. In essence, the Christian apocalyptic vision, traditionally an eschatology, now centered in the individual, in quest of his own kingdom of God within.[39]

As Miller recognized, Abrams' study operated within a view of the essential unity of Western culture, a unity that is fragmented and brought back to unity again. So magisterial and so integrated an account of the literary past and present troubled Miller. In his new analysis he used Nietzsche and Derrida to appropriate the poststructuralist perspective. Instead of continuity he described rupture, breach, tension, a Western culture at war with itself, a collapse where unity once apparently prevailed.[40]

Miller located several roots of this cultural hemorrhage, but the problem of language emerged as the most crucial. In Abrams' account, Miller wrote, "language is taken for granted as the straightforward mirror of an interchange between mind and nature, or between mind, nature, and God." But language, Miller contended, was basically metaphorical. He paraphrased Nietzsche: "Language is from the start fictive, illusory, displaced from any direct reference to things as they are." He added: "The human condition is to be caught in a web of words which weaves and reweaves for man through the centuries the same tapestry of myths, concepts, and metaphorical analogies, in short the whole system of Occidental metaphysics." We cannot free ourselves from this bondage to signs and to "the fictions they have such power to perpetuate," Miller added.[41]

Miller now saw in Abrams naive literalness. "A literary or philosophical text, for Abrams, has a single, unequivocal meaning," he said. Miller now understood language to be inescapably evasive and contradictory, replete with multiple, ambiguous meanings.[42]

Miller's essay was a signal of the American opening to continental influences in the understanding of literature. But it reflected certain American themes, too. In dismantling Abrams' great, unified Western tradition by invoking Derrida and Nietzsche, Miller carefully warned of the dangerously deterministic assumptions of Abrams' intellectual drama. Must one assume, Miller asked, that all the powerful voices of romanticism were chained to a schematic totality as controlling as that depicted by Abrams? He felt compelled to ask: "Would it be possible, by any conceivable regimen, exercise, study, or violence, to free oneself from the scheme? What would it be like to be liberated? What tools might be used to win freedom?"[43] Miller's review, secondly, hinted at the answer he would make with greater force in his later writings. To break this deterministic hold one had to retreat to the free linguistic play of texts, to their openness, to their own indeterminacy. He would enlist Nietzsche and Derrida for traditional American values and purposes.

One of Miller's exemplary essays in the poststructuralist mode was his 1976 piece on the American poet Wallace Stevens. Analyzing Stevens' poem "The Rock," Miller found a wide array of words "uncanny with antithetical and irreconcilable meanings." A word like "rock" can appear to have a solid fixed meaning, and yet be "a treacherous abyss of doubled and re-doubled meanings." In fact, Miller argued, the critic legitimately discovers hidden energies in the text, ones obscured even to the author. The status of the author dissolves in this decentering process; the text writes, "deconstructs" itself. In this way, too, a poem "calls forth potentially endless commentaries." Indeed, a mark of its greatness, Miller believed, may be the richness of such diverse interpretations. A reader may thus pursue meaning through a labyrinth that yields no center, only blind alleys and an eventual abyss.[44]

On the literary Left, Miller's appropriation of poststructuralism became suspect. Critics of the Yale School accused it of formalism, of removing literature from its social and political connections. These charges, of course, conveyed a political bias. Against the claim that he, Derrida, and de Man had yielded a sterile formalism and an elitist account of literature, Miller replied in a way that reinforced the accusations. He maintained that the new critical theory laid the foundation for a careful reading of texts that would prevent their easy absorption by sociological methods. If literature can be so easily "historicized" it will no longer be taken seriously, he insisted. "In our desire to make the study of literature count," wrote Miller, "we are always in danger of misplacing that role, of claiming too much for literature, for example, as a political or historical force. . . . Sociological theories of literature which reduce it to being a mere 'reflection' of dominant ideologies in fact tend to limit its role to that of passive mirroring, a kind of unconscious anamorphosis of the real concerns of power."[45] Do we perceive here an echo of the earlier New Criticism, with its hermetic textualizing, as some charged? If so, it was an admixture of New Criticism and poststructuralism, as indicated in Miller's conclusive statement: "The teaching of literature must be based on a love for language, a care for language and for what language can do. The study of literature must begin with language and remain focused there."[46]

For those critics, American and European, who wished to read poststructuralism more deterministically, Miller's conversion seemed incomplete. One critic considered Miller an aesthetic humanist, a Victorian in the tradition of Matthew Arnold and Walter Pater. This criticism also tried to read in the Yale School a political position, or in fact, an apolitical position. It privileged art while avoiding all the unpleasant problems of American life in the era of the Vietnam War, it was said.[47] Marxists insisted on seeing literature within a hegemonic capitalist culture. They tried to draw attention to its institutional place in the power structure of the whole society. The American literary establishment, so far as the Yale School spoke for it, reclaimed literature's autonomy. Poststructuralism's fragmenting and decentering of the literary work defied the totalizing concepts of society that had become triumphant in Western Marxism. Yale poststructuralism seemed the antithesis of any hegemonic notions of literature's role.

The Yale school had diverse voices. One scholar, in considering the critical works of Geoffrey Hartman, thought it appropriate to quote from the nineteenth-century French novelist Gustave Flaubert: "Style in itself [is] an absolute manner of seeing things." Flaubert stood in the French tradition of aestheticism and once fancied writing a book wholly "emancipated" from nature and any externals, one of pure expression, of "pure Art." This commentator located in Flaubert's wish the essence of Hartman's poststructuralist achievement. "Style," he said, "marks for Hartman the space of literature, the domain where the subject remains recoverable and alive."[48]

Hartman was born in Frankfurt, Germany in 1929. Nazi persecution of the Jews drove him to England at the age of nine and in 1946 he joined his mother in the United States. Hartman graduated from Queens College in New York City and earned his Ph.D. in comparative literature at Yale in 1953. After military service he returned to Yale, departed for stays at Iowa and Cornell, and rejoined Yale in 1967. His early interest in Wordsworth remained a lifelong attraction, and from this concentration he derived many of his critical works and formulations. In books and collections of essays—*Beyond Formalism and Other Essays* (1970), *The Fate of Reading and Other Essays* (1975), *Criticism in the Wilderness* (1980), and *Saving the Text: Literature/Derrida/Philosophy* (1981)—Hartman became a major American medium of the new critical theories. His elliptical and elusive style of writing seemed to befit the poststructuralist mode itself and his colleague Miller once referred to "the exuberant word play of Geoffrey Hartman."[49]

In a 1975 essay Hartman made a direct approach to French literary theory, assessing its impact to date and the challenges, but especially the opportunities, it posed. On matters of the authorial subject, intention and meaning in writing, and the logocentric unity of language, Derrida, said Hartman, had posed the strongest challenge yet. We confront "a language-determined indetermination," he said, and, ultimately, "the seeming impotence of traditional humanistic philosophies."[50] But in this and other essays, Hartman showed how to meet the challenge.

Deconstruction, Hartman urged, offered fresh new openings for the experience of literature. He rebelled against explication-centered criticism ("puerile or at most pedagogic"). Continental theories help us resist the specificity of literature, he said. The demise of traditional humanism, Hartman believed, exposed literature to totalizing ideologies and "quasi-religious" formulations. They imposed on it particular political readings. Deconstruction defended against the manipulation and overdetermination of literature. Granted that the arbitrary quality of language may have its abuses, all the more important, then, was rigor and responsibility by all users of words.[51]

Nevertheless, Hartman pleaded for a creative criticism. The critical essay, he wrote, aspires "to be literature and not only about it."[52] Language for Hartman was a malleable medium of art, and its very indeterminacy the basis of its rich and welcome potentiality for the critic. Indeed, the critic's work, he said, will be a "fusion of creation with criticism." "Each work of art, and each work of reading, is potentially a demonstration of freedom . . . a mode of expression that is our own." Hartman's use of poststructuralism constituted borrowing a concept, not a methodology. Indeterminacy did not yield an abyss. Rather, for Hartman, "indeterminacy is the beginning, the place where the critic, having broken loose from the shackles of univocal meaning, assumes his freedom, his creative license."[53] In the German-born Hartman we have the French reconstruction of language written in the American prose of William James.

Hartman thus did not fall into a selfless aestheticism. Criticism opened up a new space for individuality and intensely personal experience. The great work of art itself always bore the stamp of creative power. Hartman was forever Wordsworthian. "The sense of an informing spirit," he wrote, " . . . is what holds us. The great work of art is more than a text. It is the 'life-blood' of a master spirit." And to a "master-spirit" a "creative response," not a mere textual decoding, is required.[54]

Hartman, for these reasons as well, could see no ultimate threat to humanism in deconstruction. "The monuments of unageing intellect," Hartman asserted, "are not pulled down. They are, anyway, so strong, or our desire is so engaged with them, that the deconstructive activity becomes part of their structure." And deconstruction's evocative power, opening to other texts locked in memory, reaches out to greater inclusiveness, a larger aesthetic wholeness. Hartman then could even call Derrida "a conservative" in literary theory.[55]

Hartman and the Yale School had no trouble winning that label "conservative" from critics on the Left. Much in the poststructuralist Hartman could be read as literature's resistance to reification. Hartman explicitly distanced texts from their objects. "There is no transparence of thing to thought," he wrote. "The meaning cannot displace the medium. A text, precisely when authentic, will not do away with itself: we never reach the luminous limit where words disappear into their objects like shadows at noon." Texts cannot, therefore, be grounded in history or correlated to time frames that subsume and contain them.[56]

By the 1970s the academic Left had come to see reactionism in any hint of literary formalism. "The difficulty with Hartman's claim for the radicality of art," wrote Michael Sprinker, "is the privilege it grants to ideas and their representation in art at the expense of social reality." Such privileging, Sprinker insisted, implicated Hartman in the social and moral rites of "late bourgeois humanism." Hartman's criticism, he said, betrayed his nostalgia for the monuments of bourgeois culture. For Sprinker, Hartman's aesthetic was reactionary, "a holding action," the perpetuation of an old hegemony.[57]

As a literary critic, Harold Bloom was unique. He gave a profoundly idio-syncratic, but always suggestive rendering of the subjects he undertook. Bloom's 1973 book *The Anxiety of Influence* prompted Yale colleague Hillis Miller to call Bloom "perhaps the most dazzlingly creative and provocative of critics writing in English today."[58] Bloom's book transformed the grounds of humanistic scholarship and its notions of tradition and influence. Literary his-tory became a battleground in which each poet enters into an Oedipal struggle with his predecessors. Creation becomes a dimension of existential angst, a play of the haunted self that must misread the dominant literary history in which it travails. In such an understanding of the poet's work, of course, self and author functioned as very real entities. To the author of *Anxiety*, the post-structuralist dissolution of the self could be only a dreary, "antihumanistic" enterprise.[59]

For Bloom, as for Hartman, the escape from literalness applied to criticism. He described effective criticism as creative "misreading." Bloom rejected the "failed enterprise" of the New Criticism and its quest to see a single poem as an entity unto itself. On these grounds, too, however, Bloom rejected decon-struction. Poetry and criticism registered the activities of individual selves. In Bloom's reading, the French poststructuralists were subverting the notion of "self" by making the self a linguistic structure. To this "humanistic loss," Bloom rejoined that "the human writes, the human thinks."[60] The humanism that Bloom invoked restored no universal minds, no metalanguages, no dis-course speaking evenly across the ages. "Power, violence, appropriation . . . are the marks of Bloom's theory," one authority wrote.[61] Discontinuity reigned throughout; but in discontinuity Bloom located freedom.

In the formulations of Paul de Man, the Yale school furnished its most unyielding deconstructionist criticism. This Belgian emigré was America's foremost Derridean. In essays that found their way into important antholo-gies—*Blindness and Insight* (1971), *Allegories of Reading* (1979), and *The Rhetoric of Romanticism* (1984)—de Man dismantled every article of the New Critics' faith and every cornerstone of humanistic confidence in the integrity of authorial presence. The quest for meaning and order, which de Man insisted must come by the most careful and close readings of text, invariably led to the collapse of apparent order and meaning. The notion of the poem as a "verbal icon" of some kind—a timeless, self-possessed structure of meaning—could not with-stand the ambiguities and tensions that close readings executed. "Form" itself was, for de Man, only an operative fiction that simply reflected the rage for order that satisfied an innate subjective urge. Reading, under the de Man imperative, takes us ever further into the labyrinth of text and its receding ver-bal maze. But the path taken does not end in fruitless search. Meanings are always there in some sense in the text, de Man argued. They need only the requisite interpretive skill to extract them.[62]

De Man became the most controversial of the American deconstructionists and for reasons that were often openly political. To the Left, de Man seemed to suggest the most dangerous consequences of textualism. Frank Lentricchia said of de Man that he muddies the historical waters hopelessly, removing literature from its economic and social situations. Thus deprived, literature lost any political resonance. The old radical dream that culture would be a revolutionary fifth column could find no nourishment here. This criticism rerouted the quest for meaning into the deeper hinterland of textual analysis.

De Man made his own reply to his critics and to their corruptions of literary purpose. It derived heavily from his own place in an existentialist perspective influenced by Nietzsche and Heidegger. The human condition, he said, is a being-unto-death, always confronting its own alienation. This Heideggerian formulation described the human situation as an intractable alienation from Being itself. Authentic existence must at least embrace this recognition, this beginning fact of human life. De Man warned against facile escapes from this condition. We too easily relocate alienation from its spiritual location into an historical situation—that is, an economic or social one. Marxism especially effects such relocation, de Man believed. It seeks to understand human life in a strictly secular way; politics overrides poetry, which gives us the true ontological differentiations of beings and Being, the true foundations of our tragic self-knowledge. De Man's aesthetic thus led him to a position that permitted no easy temporal transcendence of our incomplete spiritual existence. Political action could never rise to the level of revealed truth. De Man's strictures about meaning in texts placed the greatest constraints on the notion of truth even in its literary location.[63]

In the judgment of some, the Yale School, with its authority and academic prestige, signaled the unsettling presence of radical ideas that dangerously eroded a stable, traditional culture. A new language of critical theory (some would say a new "jargon," a new "lingo") seemed to be rewriting the traditional humanistic language with which American students had long become familiar as part of their collegiate experiences. New uncertainties about meaning, authorial intention, reference, and subject, as Yale scholarship displayed, seemed to indicate that a morning of radical skepticism about literature had dawned, that the French had left their unsettling mark.

On the other hand, some interpreters, equally critical, perceived more traditional American habits in the Yale translations of the French. A beginning major effort to appraise the American reception of the French incursion was Frank Lentricchia's 1980 book *After the New Criticism*. A highly useful summary of post-New Critical turns in literary theory—existentialist, phenomenological, structuralist, and poststructuralist—the book gave special attention to the Yale School. Lentricchia saw in the "Yale Derrideans" the persistence of an American formalist tradition in criticism, a bad tradition. For formalism, he believed, turned culture into a mode of aesthetic pleasure (Lentricchia quoted Hartman's reference to "1001 nights of literary analysis"), hedonism. It radically severed literary texts from their social settings and isolated their authors into meaningless autonomy disguised and celebrated as individual freedom.

The Yale School, furthermore, merely found ways to shore up "the great texts," as its preoccupation with major romantic poets suggested. No new challenges to the established canon existed here, said Lentricchia. And in a striking paragraph Lentricchia lamented that the Yale scholars merely reflected, because they had in essence absorbed, the most damning aspects of American capitalist culture. To this extent, the aesthetic priorities of that group actually reflected the dominant social psyche of American life itself.

> The activity of the literary critic, thus aestheticized, thus "affectivized," does not isolate him from the mainstream conditions of modern society, but rather constitutes an academic elaboration and intensification of them. American poststructuralist literary criticism tends to be an activity of textual privatization, the critic's doomed attempt to retreat from a social landscape of fragmentation and alienation. Criticism becomes, in this perspective, something like an ultimate mode of interior decoration whose chief value lies in its power to trigger our pleasures and whose chief measure of success lies in its capacity to keep pleasure going in a potentially infinite variety of ways.[64]

In its American disciples, Lentricchia lamented, the deconstructionist assault on the props of bourgeois humanism simply resurfaced as the pleasure principles of late capitalism.

The academic debates reviewed here may suggest to some the tendency of postindustrial cultural to engage heavily in theorization. Indeed, around American university literature departments, those who indulged in poststructuralist activities were said to validate "theory" and those who criticized poststructuralism were assumed to be practicing "resistance to theory." But however esoteric these engagements often appeared, they could, as we have observed, carry considerable political baggage. The discussion to this point has hinted occasionally at the social and political implications of these linguistic and aesthetic matters. For the American Left the poststructuralist opening had some profound consequences, as Chapter Three will discuss.

three

Reading Left

The 1960s promised a radical moment in American history. The civil rights movement yielded black nationalism and urban violence. Opposition to the war in Vietnam moved from the campuses to disquieting witness in suburban living rooms. Widespread skepticism about American values and national purpose rose to possibly unprecedented heights. The likelihood of an expanded leftist opposition seemed even greater than in the Great Depression, for the 1960s also produced a substantial counterculture. When Republican parents joined their teenage children at the movie theater to see *The Graduate*, something had changed. The counterculture had its days in New York and San Francisco; but it also played in Peoria.

Then at the moment of its greatest apparent triumphs, the Left started to crack up. The 1967 convention of the Students for a Democratic Society collapsed in almost meaningless ideological warfare. Its violent wing, the Weathermen, blew up more of its own than it did capitalist banks. The bombing of Sterling Hall at the University of Wisconsin at Madison in August 1970 sent a sobering chill across the nation. Meanwhile, boisterous rock fests became scenes of drugs and death—Altamont Speedway, near San Francisco, 1969. The counterculture could seem innocent enough in the breezy ruminations of a Harvard professor; it showed its destructive side in the deaths of popular rock stars and countless incautious zealots. The Charles Manson murders finally reminded people that "dropping out" did not signify a retreat into bucolic communalism. In the end, the New Left proved correct about one thing—all the elements of social and cultural negation, all the elements of protest and resistance, could be easily absorbed by the capitalist system itself. The "Pepsi Generation" showed that. And when one visited swank Water Tower Place in the Chicago of the mid-'70s and observed the visiting suburban women wearing mink stoles and designer jeans, one knew that the "system" had co-opted the revolution.

Disappointments for the Left came also from its own misplaced expectations. People's revolutions in Cambodia brought the mass atrocities of the Khmer Rouge. The oppressive regime that created the "boat people" of Vietnam hardly confirmed faith that Third World communism might bring about a decent society. Mass movements rising against the long years of Western colonialism brought resurgent Islamic fundamentalism or succumbed to bitter ethnic and tribal warfare. They did not augur well for principles of tolerance, dissent, democratic pluralism, or women's rights.

The New Left's achievements included an enduring cultural shift that affected Americans far beyond the 1960s, however much it inspired a countermovement in the 1970s and afterward. It also included some significant theoretical advancements, especially the work of the Frankfurt School. Max Horkheimer, Walter Benjamin, Theodore Adorno, and Herbert Marcuse had significantly fortified Marxist theory by redefining the practices of oppression in advanced industrial societies. And now, as defeat at the level of politics and economics disillusioned many on the Left, culture emerged as the key playing field of any viable leftist program. Furthermore, amid the ruins of age-old dreams like intellectuals-and-workers' alliances, leftist thinkers seized the arena where they believed they could be prime movers. The American university, where the former campus newspaper editors became the tenured radicals of humanities and social science departments, emerged as the citadel of leftist opinion. In the 1970s, the New Left transformed itself into the Academic Left.[1]

Marxism in particular gained some reinforcements. For several decades in Europe, influential Marxist intellectuals had been effecting some shifts in Marxist thought. These thinkers included the Frankfurt group that relocated to the United States in the 1930s. "Western Marxism" built on the early humanist writings of Karl Marx, discovered in the late 1920s, and on the works of individuals such as Antonio Gramsci, Ernst Bloch, Georg Lukács, and Karl Korsch. They gave particular attention to the cultural complex of bourgeois society. They moved away from the strict economic determinism of Friedrich Engels, Karl Kautsky, and Georgi Plekhanov and the strict formulations of the Second International. To the humanist Marxists the relations of "base," or economic foundations, and "superstructure," the cultural and ideological constructions in a given social arrangement, appeared more complex than the older dogmatism allowed. Western Marxism acquired hybrid nomenclature—"phenomenological Marxism," "existentialist Marxism," "structuralist Marxism"—reflective of its new humanistic and cultural focus.

In Western Marxism, the notion of "totality" had particular importance and supplies a theoretical center for discussing leftist intellectual history in the 1970s. Totality had several meanings in Marxist writings. "Normative" totality expressed the Marxist ideal of a fully integrated society that overcomes alienation. "Descriptive" totality conveyed an epistemological conviction that particulars have meaning only as part of a complex whole. It contrasted with bourgeois ideals of the autonomous individual and the value system that underscores this reality in the economic system. Lukács, for example, located the distinguishing trait of bourgeois intellectuals in their inability to think holistically. Bourgeois culture seemed, in the judgment of Western Marxists, to validate notions of selfhood, individuality, separation, and fragmentation. Analytic and rationalist habits of thought, Western Marxists asserted, constructed a reality thus splintered and fractured. In opposition, Marxism normalized an opposing intellectuality that stressed unity, integration, and co-optation, each contributing to Marxism's idea of totality. As Martin Jay has written, "it is to the concept of totality that we can look for a compass to study the vast and unchartered intellectual territory that is Western Marxism."[2]

Among the Western Marxists, Antonio Gramsci had particular influence in the 1970s. A Marxist historian in 1967 could lament that among the American Left Gramsci's name was virtually unknown.[3] In the 1970s, however, no fewer than nine scholarly studies of his ideas appeared in the United States and Great Britain. Gramsci's communist loyalties had landed him in an Italian prison in 1926. His internment writings made him an original contributor to twentieth-century Marxism. He wrote some three thousand pages before his release in 1936, the year before his death. He became the patron saint of the Italian Communist Party that emerged from the antifascist movement and the publication of his works (including the six-volume edition of his prison notes and letters) assured his significance.

Gramsci displayed a holistic way of thinking. What some have called his "radical historicism" signified his effort to contextualize completely. He described the historical moment by its special inclusiveness and self-containment. It allowed no transcendent ideology to explain it. He even discounted philosophical materialism as dogmatic ideology. All products of mind, all indices of culture, for example, convey a precise historical function, Gramsci believed. We must not see them as merely epiphenomenal, he insisted. Gramsci thus sought to understand the whole social process as practically organized by specific and dominant meanings and values. Leisure, art, and entertainment also figured in this hegemony, he said, a total shaping environment that defines, as it emanates from, the prevailing arrangements of power and control. The privileged classes, Gramsci insisted, had always secured a position of hegemony in the intellectual and the political spheres. Culture always played "ideological" roles.[4]

Gramsci's reconfiguration of Marxism had the effect of narrowing the base and enlarging the superstructure that Marx at first posited. Gramsci prepared the shift from economics and politics to culture as the focus of interest in leftist intellectuals in the 1960s and more so in the 1970s. The concept of hegemony took root as a major point of discussion in literary and historical studies in Europe and the United States. It focused attention on how ruling classes maintain power by the vehicle of dominant cultural forms. Gramsci had also hoped that the proletarian cause might gain from the creation of a counter-ideology—a new hegemony fashioned by intellectual class leadership.[5]

Gramsci had a major American disciple in the historian Eugene Genovese. Born in Brooklyn in 1930, Genovese attended Brooklyn College and Columbia. He joined the Communist Party, but it dismissed him for insufficient obeisance. Nonetheless, Genovese committed himself to Marxist scholarship and became its major voice in the American historical profession in the 1970s. His outspoken opposition to the Vietnam War produced a major academic freedom case at Rutgers in 1965, though Genovese himself, however, stood athwart the more militant radical wing among the historians, and sometimes denounced it. Genovese's many briefs for Marxist scholarship made him a central figure because he tied them directly to the larger radical political cause and contributed significant studies that reflected his Marxist perspective.

Genovese specifically invoked Gramsci's authority. He judged Gramsci's idea of hegemony "perhaps his most important contribution to Marxist political theory." Genovese understood hegemony to mean a way of life and thought in which one concept of reality gains a tacit consent throughout society, that is, in its various institutional and personal expressions. It thus informs all taste, moral codes, religion, and political norms and so governs all social relations. Genovese further noted that hegemony acquires its dominance by consent, not force. In a pronunciation that very much affected his own historical studies, Genovese wrote: "The success of a ruling class in establishing its hegemony depends entirely on its ability to convince the lower classes that its interests are those of society at large—that it defends the common sensibility and stands for a natural and proper social order." For Genovese, American Marxists had focused too much on economic deprivation and political repression. They had too much faith that these conditions could produce resistance and revolution. Gramsci's notion of hegemony, he believed, could explain why they had not.[6]

The slave society and plantation life of the antebellum South supplied a natural condition to test and illustrate the operations of hegemony. Genovese's work of the late 1960s, *The Political Economy of Slavery* (1967) and *The World the Slaveholders Made* (1969), described the impact of the planter ideology within the extended class system, white and black, in the antebellum South. His book of 1974, *Roll, Jordan, Roll: The World the Slaves Made* carried hegemony a step further. This work, a national best-seller, described the role of reciprocity in master-slave relations. Slavery now became a study in human dynamics wherein pockets of resistance form but are contained within the system. Genovese described how masters contrived incentives and award systems within the routines of slave life, enabling a system of paternalism to allow slaves to assert themselves as human beings.

In impressive chapters, Genovese showed how even the cruelty and harshness of the slave system, which might have raised a destabilizing opposition against it, could recur to the enhancement of the masters. Thus, he described, slaves took recourse from oppressive overseers or drivers by appealing to the gentlemanly and Christian character of the master. They gained some relief from an owner who needed to see himself as a bearer of those virtues. There followed the ironic result that the very source of the slaves' oppression became their relief from its terrible burden. Also, Genovese explained, black Christianity, as well as folktales and music, and family life and marriage customs, supplied critical locations of self-worth, but within a framework that accepted planter domination.[7]

Genovese urged that one see things holistically. His defense of that practice made him a key voice in issues that agitated the history profession in the late 1960s and 1970s. Genovese faulted other Marxists for their limited vision of slavery and other problems in American history. They had a too simplistic notion of class, he believed, or they focused too narrowly on those at the bottom of the social ladder. Such attention might be born of genuine sympathy or of an attempt to get at a more exact truth. Thus, Marxist historian Herbert Aptheker wrote that if one wants to know what slavery was really like, one had to go to the slave; "there is the *objective* picture of that institution," he wrote.[8]

Genovese found such sentiments too simplistic. He carried that charge against a group of historians he labeled "left-liberal." Whatever the appropriateness of that label, Genovese was turning attention to an important shift among American historians in the 1960s and 1970s. The new social historians concentrated on individuals and groups in America who left no, or only sparse, written records. The project held exciting possibilities. It also carried definite political connotations. Social history of this kind proclaimed itself anti-elitist and democratic. It celebrated its efforts to give a new visibility to neglected Americans—blacks, workers, rural and mountain people, immigrants and migrant workers—the voices of the inarticulate as far as previous history went. Furthermore, social history often meant "quantitative history," the use of a complex of statistical devices to analyze social patterns—from voting to social mobility. If the masses could not speak, they could at least be counted. Practitioners of the new methodologies believed they were rewriting the American past in a new progressive mode.

American social history in these years owed much to the pioneering work of the so-called French *Annales* school. In studies by Marc Bloc and Ferdinand Braudel, attention on great historic eras shifted from the chronicles of kings and princes to the rich tapestry that interweaves humans and their environments. Along with collective "mentalities" we have the thick material culture and sensual milieu of historical eras. Braudel's works had English translations in the early 1970s and they reinforced another, more immediate influence, the work of British historian E. P. Thompson. Thompson's book, *The Making of the*

English Working Class (1963), had great appeal, especially to historians on the Left, for Thompson had won his stripes in good causes at home. Thompson wanted to invigorate Marxist history and break from some of its reductive habits.

These influences raised problems in reading Marx and placed Genovese again at the center of conflict in the profession. Genovese welcomed the rich, descriptive writings of the French historians, and he appreciated their "evocation of a total ecology." But he appraised their total contribution rather skeptically. Genovese, in an essay written with wife Elizabeth Fox-Genovese, perceived the influence of structuralism in the *Annales* school. That influence, "with its anthropological, ecological, and archeological predilections," had the effect, the Genoveses believed, of negating the historical process. It deflated the dialectics of struggle and exploitation that prevail in any given historical moment. But more important, the authors believed, the new social history among American scholars was having unwelcome effects. It had led these scholars to lavish loving affection on the isolated particulars in the lives of the oppressed peoples they studied. These "privatizing" tendencies so narrowed the field of vision as to displace the political, that is, the class struggle. The efforts to fashion a history from the bottom up, in short, betrayed a "paternalist ethos." It sought to salvage whatever space could be reclaimed from the domination of the ruling class—festivals and folk culture, domestic interiors, child-rearing and family life. But, said the Genoveses, it deprived history of its dialectic—its Marxist core—and constituted what the authors called "the political crisis of the social sciences."[9]

And, in what surely conveyed some *ad hominem* ingredients, the Genoveses politicized their case against liberal social history. They charged that much of the new genre betrayed the despair of tired radicals who had given up on politics. Determined to salvage what little they could from the great lost cause, they clung to these patches of unspoiled and uncorrupted life that managed to defy immersion into the whole. The Genoveses bristled at this fruitless and self-indulgent recourse, this "sentimental neoantiquarianism." And, to score even bigger points, they denounced this device of a "mythical autonomy" as the work of "bourgeois" habits of mind. Statistical studies signified to them the reign of fact and sanctioned the empirical realities they described. The lapse into detail, into microscopic analysis, focused on people worthy of sympathy, the Genoveses said. That habit, however, actually emulated the bourgeois intellect, with its propensity to fracture reality and prevent us from seeing it whole. The "left-liberal" historians in this way missed the interconnectedness and mutuality of class relations. In missing this essential characteristic, the Genoveses believed, one misses hegemony and its service in the perpetuation of the master classes.[10]

In the late 1960s and early 1970s these issues could not be simply "academic." Genovese, in fact, employed the concept of hegemony against the radical wing in the history profession. In 1969 he had vitriolically denounced a group of radical and thoroughly countercultural historians. They wanted to tie the American Historical Association to a clear antiwar position and denounced American institutions in toto. Staughton Lynd spoke most forcefully for this group, while Genovese and Christopher Lasch spoke for the other leftist position. A debate about the American university most clearly illustrated the opposing positions. The countercultural radicals included the university among the co-opted institutions of the United States. It had now become a force for war and capitalism, they said. They belittled the pretenses of neutral scholarship and avowedly looked for the complete radicalization of the universities. Opposing groups jockeyed for power within the AHA. R. R. Palmer outpolled Lynd for the presidency of the organization in 1969; Genovese won election to that position in 1978.[11]

Genovese came to the defense of the traditional university as a place for scholarship free of ideology or partisanship. His interest had its own political ends in view. Genovese believed that the university afforded leftist intellectuals their one haven from the controlling capitalist culture. He could see only "stupidity, envy, and malice" in the radicals' turn on the universities and in their cloying demands for "relevance." The university had far more serious business to attend to, Genovese replied. He reminded his leftist colleagues that much of the theoretical work of the international socialist movement had come out of the universities. For Genovese, theory mattered. The intellectual Left must answer the Gramscian call, he believed. It must, by the most painstaking and meticulous scholarship, forge, footnote by footnote, the rival world view that would challenge the hegemonic ideology of the ruling class. Wrote Genovese: "The responsibility of socialist intellectuals, especially those in the universities, is to get on with their work of fashioning a world view appropriate to the movement and society they wish to see born. No intellectual effort, no matter how modest, small, or removed from day-to-day politics, is irrelevant."[12] The Marxist hope now looked to the trusteeship of the intellectual classes, the Gramscian makers of the revolution.

Leftist politics also made a visible entry into literary scholarship. The early 1970s, building on the radical movement of the previous decade, saw a determined group of leftist intellectuals try to impose on the teaching of literature a program born of antiwar, anticapitalist, and countercultural partisanship. These commitments were often informed by Western Marxism and books by English Marxists Raymond Williams (*Marxism and Literature*, 1977) and Terry Eagleton (*Marxism and Literary Criticism*, 1976). But the emergence of post-structuralist theory had a dramatic impact on Marxism in France and posed a critical challenge to its American adherents.

We might better understand this politics of the word with a brief review of Marxist aesthetics. First, as noted in the previous chapter, Marxism opposed formalist understandings of art and literature. It denied that these enterprises stood apart from ordinary human experience. No such autotelic activity divorced aesthetic work from other kinds of work. We can understand art, Marxists said, only in terms of its inseparable social connections. They established its place within the entire network of productivity that prevailed in a particular historical situation. Raymond Williams wrote: "Every specific art had dissolved into it, at every level of its operations, not only specific social relations, which in a given phase define it . . . but also specific means of production, on the mastery of which its production depends."[13]

Second, to the extent that aesthetics inherits ideas of formalism, it reflects the lasting influence of bourgeois culture. In nearly every Marxist account, formalism is rendered a species of bourgeois ideology. Marxism also understands formalism as a bourgeois device to create a dualism of "art" versus "production," or mere "work," that obscures the oppressive contradictions of capitalism. Privileged terms such as "truth," "beauty," "the universal," and "taste" have clearly idealist, but emphatically hegemonic functions. They are the means by which the ruling economic classes connect themselves to a protective and sacrosanct cultural order.[14]

Third, even among Marxists who stress the critical, the negating, or the utopian power of art, the place of the subject, the creator, is reduced. An author, it is said, is already a socialized being, carrying the weight of a specific historical time and condition. Even the contents of consciousness, it was sometimes argued, were social productions. This fact maintains even to the extent that oppositional art "deforms" its world and thus exposes its contradictions; it is nonetheless socially derived. In Marxist literary criticism one hears little about the creative power of individual artists or writers. To acknowledge "genius," it seems, threatens to propel us back into all the trappings of bourgeois individualism.[15]

Fourth, all these points show why, even to oppositional theorists like the Frankfurt School, the idea of totality remained an important Marxist concept. Marxists always sought a wider referentiality for the aesthetic. In reaction to bourgeois culture, they sought to dilute its special and privileged meanings into a more comprehensive complex of social class. They wanted to tie it to networks of production, cultural institutions, and media of exchange. Western Marxism moved away from rigid notions of "reflection" and stressed "mediation" instead. That idea confirmed the "totality" of the social and cultural complex, thus making discussions of art and literature all the more serious as political subjects.

In 1969, literary scholar Frederick Crews spoke to a forum of the Modern Language Association (MLA). He challenged the reigning scholarly practices of this mammoth academic organization. His comments appeared later in the journal of this group under the title "Do Literary Scholars Have an Ideology?" The essay immediately became controversial. Answering his own question, Crews affirmed that literary studies exercise an ideology even when they vehemently disavow any such intention. Whether as formalism, objectivity, scientific scholarship, or universalistic humanism, Crews argued, the study of literature in the American college and university carried a hidden agenda that made the literary establishment a reactionary institution.

Crews' argument rested on some facile assumptions about American capitalism. Capitalism, he argued, serves predominantly for large investors who habitually turn to the state to extricate themselves from the dilemmas that the system creates. All institutions, Crews averred, and no less so the college and university, exist to further the interests of the whole system. Furthermore, this unholy alliance, Crews said, had forced onto institutions of higher learning a certain mode of scholarly practice. Its value-free pretensions forestalled in it any ideological challenge to the existing order. Its empirical standards, he added, made it fact-oriented, limited to parts and ignorant of the historical and social totality of American capitalist society. Literary studies, more particularly, Crews believed, had fallen into a formalistic concern with end products. They dealt with the hermetic inner text and executed "an escape clause" from the real world. They thus dangerously ignored Georg Lukács' instruction that literature always has class meaning. Criticism confined to formalistic analysis, Crews insisted, only too well suits a society comfortable in its material affluence and complacent about its patterns of domination.[16]

Crews carried his attack even into the matter of scholarly style. Capitalism, in its monopoly phase, he said, requires not a scholarship of commitment and passion, but one of manipulation, of dexterous deployment of analytical skills and investigation. Such a preoccupation, Crews said, neuters whatever oppositional force might find its way into art. The passion of a writer, even the rage and indignation that once inspired a novel or poem, now dissolves before the "cold and subtle strategy" of the detached, scientific observer. Literature thus again loses its political relation.[17]

More dramatic was the case of Louis Kampf. At the MLA's 1968 convention in New York, Kampf and two graduate students got themselves arrested in the lobby of the American Hotel. The event followed a skirmish with hotel guards over the insurgents' efforts to mount posters of the New University Conference. The New University included SDS alumni and others who wished to push universities in a radical direction. They sought to expose higher education's complicity in fostering war and oppression. They also hoped to promote radical scholarship that would further New Left goals. The arrest of Kampf and his affiliates became an immediate cause célèbre. Kampf even rode his unexpected attention to election as second vice-president of the MLA and succession thereafter to the presidency in 1971.[18]

Kampf's office gave him a forum to set forth his views on literature and the academic profession. He outlined them in a presidential address that appeared in *PMLA* in 1972. Kampf betrayed no ambiguity in his message. Literary study, he said, is now part and parcel of an academic structure that sits comfortably within the segmented and rationalized structure of capitalist society. "Indeed," wrote Kampf, "the division and subdivision of knowledge is one cultural product of capitalism's need for rationalization." Language departments, products of a rationalization of knowledge, represent, said Kampf, ideological components of a system that feeds on itself by its own logic of integration. They proved to Kampf the reactionary role of formal academic learning. Scholarship is "individualistic, competitive, and privatized," he said. We must now forge a new agenda, a broader literary curriculum addressing human and social need.[19]

Kampf's views did not by any means speak for most literary academics. But never before, probably, had traditional academic ideas and practices faced such systematic opposition. The partisans of reform occupied positions at "prestigious" American universities. And this group had a further augmentation of its position in the middle 1970s when Richard Ohmann published *English in America: A Radical View of the Profession*. Ohmann acknowledged his indebtedness to Kampf and to the Radical Caucus in English and the Modern Languages.

Ohmann maintained that literature exercised two influences. One was conservative and tradition-affirming, the other radical, critical, and potentially revolutionary in its impact. The academic literary profession, he charged, systematically obscured the critical power of literature. It did so through special connivance. All the schools of "bourgeois" criticism, Ohmann maintained, presented literature as a phenomenon apart, detached from the associated realities of commerce, politics, science, and technology. Literature, as taught, aspired to lift its audience into a timeless "tradition" removed from these realities. Ohmann, however, insisted that literature emerges as a product of specific historical conditions, and as a judgment and critique of those conditions. But the dominant formalism of English departments renders them parts of a harmless and transcendent humanism. What society received from their literary scholars in their academic institutions answered precisely their expectations: a normative, sustaining tradition of letters that supported the social order and dispelled critical thinking.[20]

These writings expressed the political passions of a revolutionary ferment and often took on a polemical and cliché-driven rhetoric. But in the realm of scholarly Marxism a sophisticated reconstruction of theory did take shape. Discussion of this undertaking would hardly be one-sided if it focuses on the contribution of one individual. Fredric Jameson, one writer has said, was "without doubt the leading Marxist critic and literary theorist of his generation in North America." Amid the often confusing crossroads of the poststructuralist reconstruction and the Marxist turn in literary theory, Jameson became the key American signpost. He merits focal attention in this chapter.

Born in Cleveland in 1934, Jameson attended school in New Jersey, took his B.A. at Haverford College, and his M.A. and Ph.D. at Yale in 1956 and 1960. His essay "Metacommentary" won a major award after its publication in *PMLA* in 1971. At the same time Jameson was doing pioneering work. His book *Marxism and Form*, published the same year as the essay, made Jameson the first American scholar to undertake a nearly comprehensive account and synthesis of Western Marxism. The study offered explanatory chapters and critical commentary on such prominent individuals in this company as Adorno, Walter Benjamin, Marcuse, Bloch, Lukács, and the individual to whom Jameson felt especially indebted, Jean-Paul Sartre. James clearly held a partisan stance toward his subjects and this work contributed to his own emerging stature within Western Marxism itself.

In 1972, Jameson published *The Prison-House of Language: A Critical Account of Structuralism and Russian Formalism.* Here again Jameson was introducing to much of his audience a whole new mode of thinking. He made the book more than a primer, however. Jameson wanted to bring the structuralist movement under a Marxist examination. With excursions into Jacques Lacan, Jacques Derrida, and other poststructuralists, Jameson became the American who sustained Marxism against the poststructuralist challenge. He had considerable resources for the task. A professor of French literature at Yale and later at Duke, Jameson drew widely from contemporary theory. Even when overburdened by too heavily Marxist rigor, his critical pieces contained fresh and engaging insights.

Jameson's writings posited an intellectual dichotomy that he perceived operating in Western thought since the seventeenth century. By the late twentieth century Jameson could describe it as an ideological opposition between an empiricist philosophy associated with Anglo-American thought and a dialectical logic now advanced by Western Marxists. (Jameson observed that a previous idealist tradition had been partially salvaged by Hegel and his followers.) To Jameson empiricism represented a reactionary mode of thinking. That intellectual habit, he said, fragmented experience by its restrictive attention to the sense data of isolated phenomena. It thereby also raised "fact" to a valorized status, a position of epistemological privilege. Empiricism as such could never foster a critical, or skeptical, frame of mind. Jameson even labeled empiricism escapist. Ultimately, this mode of thinking, he believed, could not embrace in its vision the full implications, the larger complexities, of any given situation. Its problem-solving inclinations must always confront the fragments of reality in a manner that could yield only piecemeal ameliorations. Jameson harbored no doubts that empiricism constituted the class ideology of the bourgeoisie.[21]

In turn, Jameson became an outright champion of dialectical thinking. From literature to politics, all hinged for him on the triumph of dialectical thinking. In making its case, Jameson could describe in uncharacteristically dramatic expression a kind of spiritual conversion. "There is a breathlessness about [the] shift from the normal object-oriented activity of the mind," he wrote, "to . . . dialectical self-consciousness—something of the sickening shudder we feel in an elevator's fall or in the sudden dip in an airliner." Taking on a dialectical view of life could be a form of "epistemological shock," Jameson said, so radical and so decisive was the break from the confinements of older intellectual habits associated with advanced technological culture.[22]

Dialectical thinking meant thinking the totality. Here Jameson forged the key link with Western Marxism. "The peculiar difficulty of dialectical writing," he wrote, "lies indeed in its holistic, 'totalizing' character: as though you could not say any one thing until you had first said everything; as though with each new idea you were bound to recapitulate the entire system."[23] This emphasis greatly informed the historicizing activity in Jameson's Marxism. To see things in historical inclusiveness, he believed, exposed the errors in traditional Western humanism, with its radical dualism of subject and object. The imperial and authoritative subject that underscores bourgeois ideology is dissolved in Marxist dialectics. It retreats into the entire social complex and loses its vaunted autonomy. Jameson believed that with the dialectical erosion of the subject, bourgeois humanist ideologies—including especially formalism in aesthetics—would lose their authority.[24]

To reassert a Marxist dialectic against bourgeois humanism was one thing. To confront a now more serious challenge was another. That challenge came from poststructuralism. In Europe, in the face of that challenge, Marxism had to make a rapid retreat. One could clearly differentiate between Marxism and postmodernism, especially in postmodernism's alienation from all totalizing ways of thinking. Postmodernists stressed decenteredness, infinite play and openness, repetition and displacement, and estrangement from all logocentric formulations. Marxism stressed unity and integration, organicism, hegemony, totality, and dialectics. Poststructuralism, one might say, fixated on holes, Marxism on wholes. Thus, in reflecting on the major voices of postmodernism—Barthes, Derrida, Lacan, Foucault, and others—Martin Jay wrote: "If one had to find one common denominator among the major figures normally included in the postmodernist category . . . it would have to be their unremitting hostility towards totality."[25]

From the 1960s on, Marxism in France went increasingly out of vogue. That unexpected development owed much to the ascendancy of Michel Foucault. Foucault studied with Louis Althusser, whose works in the 1960s made some important departures in Marxist theory and influenced it in a postmodernist direction. Foucault's historical writings reflect something of that influence but his ingenious accounts of social structures, of asylums and prisons, for instance, made him quite a singular force.

Foucault completed *Surveiller et Punir* in 1975 and its English translation followed in *Discipline and Punish: The Birth of the Prison* in 1977. As Foucault had done with his studies of discursive systems and intellectual "genealogies," so also in his focus on institutions he found destabilizing activities wherever order appeared to prevail. Power and authority for him always had multiple and ubiquitous locations. He found it exercised but never possessed, as much an ascending phenomenon as descending. In Foucauldian analysis, binary oppositions between ruling classes and subordinate classes become highly attenuated, and as such they call the assumed class basis of power into question. Foucault shared with Marxists an emphatic historicity and a diachronic perspective on all things. But Foucault greatly complicated the Marxian dialectic of ruling class and oppressed class. He perceived in all systems and structures a multiplicity of micropowers and a plurality of irregular oppositions that constantly shifted and regrouped.[26]

One could describe the later Foucault as a postmodernist historian or sociologist. What he was effecting in his studies paralleled the decentering and antisytematizing assaults made by the postmodernist literary theorists in their own domain. For example, in writing about power and the state, Foucault did not attribute any "essence" to the state. The state is only a composite result of vast localities of power and their interactions, he believed, a multiplicity of centers and mechanisms. Nor is power, in the state or elsewhere, merely a device of control. Alan Sheridan summarized Foucault's conception of power in this way:

> Power is not to be seen as subordinate to some other factor. It does not exist simply to enforce economic exploitation: it does not play the role of superstructure to an economic infrastructure. Power is already present at the very inception of the modes of production: it constitutes its very structure. Power has no finality, but responds to particular problems, combining not in a totalized, centralized, manner, but by serial repercussion. Power is not simply repressive; it is also productive.[27]

Foucault himself embraced a leftist political position. His challenge to Marxism has special interest in that regard. Foucault, for one, considered Marxism intellectually antiquated. He wrote, "Marxism exists in nineteenth-century thought like a fish in water: it is unable to breathe anywhere else."[28] For Foucault, expressive totalities such as Marxism were a reflex of the older intellectual habits that he now exposed. Marxism, with its habit of centering power and tracing its diffusions into the social whole, betrayed the rage to impose order and unity, and a process of change, onto a reality that had no such containments. Marxism, with its logocentric debt to Hegel, represented intellectual atavism.

In France, by the middle 1970s, the Foucauldian revolution was bringing Marxist influence to nil. Foucault had produced a non-Marxist, albeit leftist paradigm, that challenged the Marxist constructs on key points, but nowhere more importantly than in its traditional ideas of totality. And from outside the Left, from the conservative *nouveaux philosophes*, for example, the assault on Marxist assumptions became acutely specific. Now anti-Marxists could trace a direct line that led from Hegel's totalistic Absolute Spirit to the Gulag of Stalinism. The teleology of the German philosopher, they said, while harmless in its idealistic formulation, is relocated in history by the Marxist adaptation and finds its brutal but inevitable end in the annulment of all contradictions as enacted by the Communist state. "Thus Absolute Spirit becomes the knock at the door, in the name of History, of the secret police."[29]

The end of the decade saw the publication of its most emblematic post-modernist work. Edward Said's remarkable study *Orientalism* demonstrated the Marxist reinforcement by poststructuralism in a powerful leftist critique. Said, the Palestinian-born scholar at Columbia, took on a subject of global dimensions. *Orientalism* dealt with familiar leftist themes—imperialism and Western power—and restated them in a dramatic new construction. After its publication in the United States in 1979, *Orientalism* received a French translation in 1980 and more in Arabic, Japanese, German, Portuguese, Italian, Spanish, Polish and several other languages in the next decade and a half. For all its strengths and weaknesses, *Orientalism* highlights the postmodernist arrival.

Said acknowledged first a debt to Gramsci, finding Gramsci's idea of hegemony "an indispensable construct for any understanding of cultural life in the industrial West."[30] He acknowledged British Marxist Raymond Williams also. But he clearly made most use of Foucault. *Orientalism* is above all a study of knowledge and power. It owes that much perhaps to the New Left, as Said in fact refers to Orientalism as the "corporate institution for dealing with the Orient."[31] Said describes in his book a massive structure of erudition, ranging from the academy to the museum to the colonial offices. It comprises anthropology, biology, language, history, and race in its intellectual imperium. And for Said there is nothing innocent at all about this venture. From the time when Napoleon brought with him in his conquest of Egypt a whole retinue of savants, Orientalism has been the manner by which the West has pursued the subjugation of that realm. "Orientalism, then," wrote Said, "is knowledge of the Orient that places things Oriental in class, court, prison, or manual for scrutiny, discipline or governing."[32]

Orientalism, though, surpasses any ordinary Marxist understanding of imperialism. Its focus is not economics but textuality. For the initial Western project respecting the Orient, Said believed, was the simple task of creating it. Like any encounter of a powerful subject with an unknown presence, the West had to fashion, to create, the Orient, this menacing "Other," before it could approach it in any effective way. Thus Said tells us: "My idea is that European and then American interest in the Orient was political . . . but it was the culture that created that interest, that acted dynamically along with brute political, economic, and military rationales to make the Orient the varied and complicated place that it obviously was in the field I call Orientalism."[33]

Said's analysis reflects Foucauldian understanding of knowledge. Orientalism, the knowledge complex, exists intimately within a geopolitical exchange emanating from pervasive Western contingencies. Thus, representation of the Orient in Orientalism cannot have a detached or disinterested character. Too much political and economic necessity drives the enterprise. In Said the key poststructuralist understanding of representation now reveals a stark and harsh political reality. For "representation" acquires far greater significance than "truth." Said takes up a stricture significant from Saussure onward—that what is important in representation is what is left out. The West cannot represent the Orient in itself, as a vital human complexity. It must reduce it, familiarize it, represent it.

> The value, efficacy, strength, apparent veracity of a written statement about the Orient therefore relies very little, and cannot instrumentally depend, on the Orient as such. On the contrary, the written statement is a presence to the reader by virtue of its having excluded, displaced, made supererogatory any such *real thing* as "the orient."[34]

Said thus concludes that the Orient is "Orientalized." It discloses to us much more about the culture and the political machinations of the West than it does of its manifest subject. And those Western habits become decisive. They include an essentialist rendering of the Orient, a critical part of the textualizing process operative in the academic disciplines. Textual mastery provides the West its enabling control, "to feel oneself as a European in command, almost at will, of Oriental history, time, and geography." Thus, wrote Said, the universe of discourse opened up by Napoleon is followed, chronologically and logically, by the Suez Canal. "Thereafter," he says, "the notion of the 'Oriental' is an administrative or executive one."[35]

The very textual flavor of Said's book was poststructuralist and some reviewers found the language burden almost unbearable— jargon-laden and obscure. But most found it a passionate work and a disturbing polemic. It impressed also by its immense erudition. Said no doubt highlighted Western abuse over Western benevolence, even neglecting to note the flourishing of Arabic Orientalism stimulated by Western scholarship. But one could agree with the reviewer who called *Orientalism* a "fierce and courageous work."[36]

Finally, Fredric Jameson again tried to make the Marxist response to postmodernism. He recognized the poststructuralist challenge to the Marxist program and the place of Derrida and Foucault in creating it. Some of his work in the early and mid-seventies led to his formidable 1981 book, *The Political Unconscious*. Jameson clearly had some misgivings about postmodernism. He faulted postmodernism for its transforming historical reality—defined by economics, political power, and historical fact—into a world of discourse. In the postmodernist view of things, he said, all seemed to dissolve into a substanceless world of unreality. In a remarkably understated passage, Jameson made a profound observation. The very raising of language to a kind of autonomous reality of its own, he said, actually registered the fragmenting and autonomizing thinking that prevailed in late capitalism. Jameson thus saw in postmodernism itself the historic situation of which it was a cultural reflection. Bourgeois culture, Jameson believed, sustained as autonomous entities those broken bits and pieces of experience, those fragments of older unities, that it now made to serve as therapeutic salve for its general dehumanizing activity.

The loss of the notion of totality under the poststructuralist aegis stands as a triumph of all in Western thought that Jameson had posed against the Marxist dialectic.[37]

Nonetheless, poststructuralism had much to suggest to Jameson. It had prepared a sustained attack on such "bourgeois" norms as the subject (the autonomous self) and formalist ideas concerning the self-enclosure of the cultural product. Jameson borrowed at key places from Althusser, and Jameson's own Marxism would now meet the postmodernist challenge by some accommodation to it. Jameson's key contribution was his idea of the political unconscious.

All cultural products, Jameson said, bear the stamp of a large operational process in the social milieu; that is, they reveal "the all-embracing unity of a single code which they must share and which thus characterizes the larger unity of the social system." This unity, Jameson added, "will be what the Marxian tradition designates as a 'mode of production.' "[38] To this extent, too, literary form is but the encoding of a materialistic process, a historical moment. That consideration must underscore all effective interpretation of literary works. For interpretation, Jameson explained, works to restore a meaning already there, a meaning at once disguised and revealed in narrative and stylistic form. Thus interpretation moves progressively, from inner content and structure, outward to the whole extended social complex.[39]

Jameson sought to prepare a decoding of literature. The literary text and its historical subtext are reread in terms of the oppositional language of social classes and the value systems ("ideologemes") that legitimate their domination. The decoding process discloses the alienating effects of capitalist domination at the same time it opens up to us the social revolution that did not occur. Literature is first and foremost the bearer of the "political unconscious," the history that is the "absent cause" (an Althusserian term)—the absent social revolution, the repressed or accommodated negation—that is in turn its shaping force.

Jamesonian interpretation thus reflects a view of literature as a kind of collective repression. We glimpse the contents of that repression only indirectly, but they nonetheless reveal to us the alienating process of capitalism and the signs of its hegemonic control. This kind of reading incorporates a postmodernist mode of analysis. Reading, under Jameson's prescription, reveals a revolutionary situation—the markings of alienation and repression. But as in Derrida, the text is always constituted by what is absent from it, so in Jameson, the cultural product is ultimately a constituent of the absent cause, the revolution that *did not* occur. This perception surely makes Jameson a key synthetic thinker, one who, in the United States and Europe, made the most important opening of Marxism to the postmodernist arrival.

How might the significance and effectiveness of the Marxist and poststructuralist shifts of the 1970s be assessed? This chapter has discussed them as challenges to each other. That fact, however, should not obscure their mutually reinforcing roles in discrediting the claims of Western humanism and their mutually reinforcing aversion to bourgeois culture. At least to that extent, both Marxism and poststructuralism advanced the intellectual Left in Europe and the United States. Did the Left itself gain by these appropriations? Gerald Graff, for one, had severe doubts.

Graff published his book *Literature Against Itself* in 1979. Writing from a position clearly sympathetic to liberal cultural politics, Graff called for a close look at what was happening on the intellectual Left and brought poststructuralism, Marxism, and other leftist views under examination. He respected their importance, at least. "As the political radicalism of the sixties has waned," he wrote, "cultural radicalism has grown proportionately in influence."[40] He also concluded that Marxist and postmodernist theorists had misconstrued the nature of their enemy and could not therefore mount an effective critique of capitalism and bourgeois culture.

The poststructuralists, Graff wrote, had constructed a highly antimimetic theory of literature. They disallowed any references from the text to an external reality and turned literature in on itself. They denied it the ability to be representational. Literature, they asserted, is not about the world; it is about itself. "There is nothing outside the text," we recall. Graff could see behind this strategy nothing but bourgeois animus. It betrayed the fear of postmodernist literary theorists that any allowing of literature to represent the real world can only return us to that world, the world rejected. Literature must be divested of authority, truth, privileged voice, and humanistic verities lest it emulate the scientific rationalism, technocratic expertise, and elitist structure of bourgeois society. "The need of the humanities to dissociate themselves from anything that might be associated with bourgeois culture," wrote Graff, "not only requires the liquidation of mimetic literary models but virtually anything of an objective truth claim, whether in literature, criticism, or any other form of discourse." Graff had little patience for this preciosity. He accused the deconstructionists of exercising "a new moralism." [41]

What the poststructuralists failed to realize, Graff insisted, was that the dominant "unreality" in our modern lives is capitalist society itself. For capitalism creates and thrives in a social milieu that destroys all substantial things. It eradicates all vestiges of tradition, all that assures continuity of life patterns and institutional familiarity. "The essence of capitalist society," said Graff, "is its unreality, its malleable, ephemeral quality."[42] Ominously, then, literary theory validates this prevailing norm by bringing literature into its domain. Poststructuralist theory, said Graff, deprives literature of its ability to reflect any substantive contents that connect it to life. Unreality becomes a kind of absolute.[43]

Here we confront a profound paradox, Graff observed. For the leftist deconstructionists merely emulate and indirectly validate the very society they wish to escape. Capitalism negates all locations of authority in order to remove all resistances to consumerism and to assure the total "reification" (commodification) of the world. Graff feared that poststructuralism had so thoroughly grounded suspicion of authority and privileged voice as to be a cooperating partner in capitalism's major enterprise. Poststructuralist theorists may fancy that they are immunizing the literary work against its assimilation into the commodity culture, Graff wrote, but they have only produced a new commodity, the autotelic literary item. The literary Left to this extent not only partakes of the larger capitalist culture; it deprives literature of any critical voice in it.[44]

Finally, Graff judged the Marxists and other literary radicals no more effective than the poststructuralists in advancing a useful criticism of capitalism. Referring to Ohmann, Graff noted his charge that the universities had become components of bourgeois culture and its scientific rationalism, the source of its systems of controls. As such, Ohmann reflected a leftist habit of seeing modern society under the hegemonic power of an all-pervasive ideology. The universities, it was charged, functioned under that controlling system. To Graff, that emphasis wholly missed the point. For observers from de Tocqueville to Marx himself had noted that capitalism has no controlling ideology, no permanent set of manners or beliefs peculiar to the capitalist "class." Graff's point even reflected a lament that some neoconservatives in the 1970s also made about corporate America. Graff wrote:

> The modern corporation has disencumbered itself from any "values" except the long-range maximization of profit, and profit will appropriate any type of values and any type of culture. The corporate spirit, far from being rigid or absolutist, is cool, opportunistic, unsentimental; it adapts to "rapidly changing times" and encourages innovation. It understands the impracticality of having any particular ideology.

If it were a mark of postindustrial society to overtheorize, Graff seemed to say, then the Left had fallen victim to one of postmodernism's own pervasive habits. For theory yields large interpretive models and descriptions and contains all, from the corporation to the university, within its holistic accounts. But in an era when surrealism more than scientific rationalism better describes capitalist society, Graff believed, theory's critical assault could never capture its elusive enemy.[45]

By a curious twist, then, Marxism caught itself in a difficult dilemma. Its tradition had taught it that capitalism imposes a controlling hegemony so severe that negation becomes highly problematic. That possibility nonetheless inspired hope that some detachment or critical distance might be effected. Radical textualism, in which language turns inward on itself and cannot reference an external reality, inspired a kind of leftist aestheticism that grounded some of the now prominent cultural Marxism of the 1970s. But that retreat, as its opponents labeled it, invited rebuke. It came most vociferously from those within the Marxist penumbra itself. They saw only the emulation of bour-geois privileging of the aesthetic object and hedonism, a *plaisir du texte*, post-modernist playfulness, bourgeois sensuality. In the boldest and most inge-nious effort at reconciling these two standards of cultural radicalism, Jameson's construction of the political unconscious produced a poststructural-ist Marxist compound. But at what cost? Marx's original manifesto of muscle and blood, after six score and ten years, had retreated into the vast interior of this buried retreat, into postindustrial amorphousness.

four

Postmodernism I, Painting

The American art world of the 1970s flourished in postindustrial pluralism and confusion. A bewildering variety of styles abounded and critics and commentators faced the formidable challenge of sorting things out and making sense of it all. The suddenness of the change overwhelmed critics. In 1971 the editor of *Art in America* commented, "the sixties are receding at such a speed they now have a period look ... How could such a decade seem, after a year of the seventies, so far away?"[1] Among the many genres that prevailed in the decade—some developing out of trends of the 1960s, others originating in the seventies—one could name the following: conceptual art, pattern and decoration, photo-Realism, light-and-space art, minimalism, narrative art, neo-expressionism, sound art, body art, "bad" painting, crafts-as-art, feminist art, fashion art, high-tech art, media art, new image, performance art, systematic abstraction, abstract illusionism, figurative expression, homoerotic art, environmental art, and post-pop art.[2] The label "pluralist" became the safest and eventually the conventional term for the overall variety of seventies art. But ultimately it did not suffice; it was too nondescript. Critics needed a more precise terminology. Indeed, it was more fun to deal with the explosion of new styles by calling it the "postmodernist" phenomenon.

If nothing else, postmodernist art longed to be at home in the world. In terms of the heavy political substance that accompanied art criticism in the 1970s, that yearning would cause postmodernist art to have both a radical and a conservative character; and it would reinforce the reigning confusion. Some discerned in postmodernism an antiart quality. Often, new artists disdained the museums and took their art into the streets, where it spoke in a new vernacular, forsaking the technicalities of high art and its formalist language. Art lost its hermetic location. It intermixed with the economy of postindustrialism

54

as it dispensed images in profusion. Indeed, art became so dispersed as to lose its distinct autonomy. A design for a record cover or billboard could show as much sophistication as a contemporary creation on a gallery wall. Now less preoccupied with the question of its peculiar essence, art intermixed with commercial culture and stood at ease with all its commonplaces.[3] As Kim Levin wrote, "the most interesting art during most of the '70s was seldom where you'd expect to find it and was often barely recognizable as 'art.' Art didn't disappear ... but it went into hiding, paradoxically, as it tried to become more accessible and move into the world."[4]

Postmodernist vernacular mixed not only with commerce but also with crafts. Into the 1950s, the divisions between art—nonfunctional, nonutilitarian—and craft seemed clearly distinct. But the dissolution of these categories that began then became well pronounced and attracted attention in the 1970s. Craftsmen began to create nonfunctioning objects barely distinguishable from sculpture, while artists took an interest in functionality, producing "artists' furniture," one of many postmodernist hybrids in the 1970s. To be sure, similar previous efforts by artists (Pablo Picasso and Constantin Brancusi) had associated arts/crafts with radical politics, but they had not won recognition as "art." Under postmodernism's relaxed assessment of what constituted "art," one critic observed, "a chair being exhibited in a gallery today ... may be the work of an artist, an architect, a furniture designer, or a craftsperson."[5]

The so-called "fashion aesthetic" also reflected the blurring of distinctions. Many artists who experimented with postmodernist styles had trained as commercial artists. Fashion aesthetic incorporated the glitz and sexiness of the fashion world, bestowing these qualities as a veneer on ordinary objects. Irving Penn's work in the 1970s gave elegance to household refuse and other typically unpalatable commonplaces such as cigarette butts. Postmodernism delighted to engage in such levelling acts. It blurred distinctions and broke down the hierarchies of our quotidian existence; garbage cans take on a glitzy sexiness. In doing so, it raised for art critics the question whether postmodernism represented a healthy antielitism or an indiscriminate democratic or populist ethic. In 1978 the prestigious Museum of Modern Art in New York (MoMA) mounted a major exhibition on fashion art.[6] And so it went, as the museums everywhere found new subjects for display. These subjects eroded the established categories of art as they dissolved the distinctions between art and life. "In the '70s," wrote Levin, "sculptors simulated architecture, painters simulated decoration, video artists simulated TV, and performance artists simulated life."[7]

Postmodernism's eclecticism also reflected a renewed interest in the past. Art history became a huge rummage sale that one could roam at will, picking here and there to rediscover forgotten and often maligned relics. Everywhere, it seemed, museums and galleries put on revivals. This movement reinforced the flight from modernism and high formalism, bringing attention to many old varieties of academic art that had been much disparaged during modernism's ascendancy in the twentieth century. Art again became ornamental. Antiquarian curiosity resurfaced. The art world seemed now to be bored with the "arctic purity" of modernism, escaping its aesthetic chill for a little sensuous but innocent indulgence. Revivalism was a measure of postmodernism's permissiveness and tolerance. If it resuscitated discredited forms of Academy art—London's Royal Academy of Arts or Paris's Académie des Beaux Arts— it did so not to reestablish old standards but to move out from under the elitist prerogatives of modernism. Since the early twentieth century, the dominant avant-garde taste had disparaged "official" art. In the curious and tolerant 1970s, it got another look. Hence, the seventies won for itself a designation as the "decade of the Neo."[8]

The "innate eclecticism of the decade"[9] left the 1970s in a situation of frustrating ambiguity. To some it "seemed like nothing happened" in the art world—no dominant new forms, no major breakthroughs, no new conceptual departures, no artist superstars. Ransacking the past did not yield any sense of chronological depth, only a perpetual present. The art vocabulary of the day failed to yield concreteness. "After the early '70s," wrote Levin, "words fail us, the glossary dissolves. The lines of influence and threads of history get so tangled together that there are no terms that really work."[10] It was "as if the whole history of styles had suddenly come unstuck," wrote critic Suzi Gablik.[11]

The fact that no single particular style tended to dominate in the 1970s signified the end of the modernist era. By decade's end, the art commentaries measured up the gains and losses in the jump from modernism to postmodernism. Critics tried to relate this dramatic shift to the concurrent social and economic transformations in America. Art commentary, in short, became politically laden, a critical battlefield offering some surprises. The politics of art will constitute the primary emphasis of this chapter.

A thorough review of the art movements and styles of the 1970s is beyond the scope of this study, but some attention to two of the trends will provide some helpful orientation.

Photo-Realism, or "Super Realism," a movement active primarily in the United States, began in the mid-sixties and flourished into the mid-seventies. This type of realist painting found its subject in the photograph, or the photographic vision of reality. It coincided with other genres that collectively expressed the return-to-the-object theme initiated by Pop Art in the 1960s. Robert Bechtle, for example, might paint from an old snapshot a family posed in front of its 1950s car and would incorporate into the scene the flattening effect of the camera on the image. Chuck Close rendered giant portrait heads that stare out at the viewer and reflect this artist's interest in how the camera distorts the image as rendered by the naive eye. In Close's case, we have an artist who broke abruptly from an earlier career in modernism. "I couldn't stand what I was doing," he said. He ceased to use other people's "art marks" and dispensed with the thick, luxurious paint of his early practice, eliminated

Chuck Close, *Keith* (1970). Acrylic on canvas, 108 × 84". *Courtesy of the Pace Gallery, New York.*

color, and used the air brush exclusively.[12] Photo-Realism provided all kinds of subject opportunities. Malcolm Morley portrayed travellers on glamorous cruise ships, his paintings replicating travel brochures.[13]

Photo-Realism did not have an easy time of it. Some considered it retroactive and banal, an idealization of suburban or middle-class America and lacking any critical posture. Photo-Realism's "blankness and emotional numbness," one critic felt, reflected the withdrawal symptoms of the Vietnam War, the

Robert Bechtle, *Berkeley Pinto* (1976). Oil on canvas, 48 × 69". *Courtesy of O.K. Harris Gallery, New York, and Gallery Paule Anglim, San Francisco.*

shell-shocked sensibility induced by that conflict.[14] Formalists resented the intrusion of the vernacular into art and recoiled from these concessions to mass culture. What was vernacular to the postmodernists was kitsch to the older critics. Photo-Realism looked in on the local, the concrete, the quotidian. It constituted "an inviting and peaceful retreat from the terrible vastness and agitation of the world," so relished by modernist painters. To its detractors, then, Super Realism conspired in the conservative reaction in American painting of the 1970s.[15] Realists held their ground. Painter Al Leslie defined his works as an effort "to put back into art all the painting the Modernists took out."[16]

The paintings of Rackstraw Downes amplify these generalities of Super Realism. Downes' interests reflected the cultural dialectics of postindustrialism. Although 1970s paintings convey a postindustrial confusion of time, they show also a countervailing recourse to space, a search for stabilizing locality and permanence. Downes was "fascinated by the local and the mundane." His work did not seek quiet withdrawal from the world; it sustained "a habitual immersion in it." Downes did not utilize interpretive strategies in approaching his subject matter, but gave his renderings more the quality of landscape documentary. His New York City settings, from Central Park to Harlem River Drive to the tennis courts at Riverside Park, provide lavish detail for the itinerant viewer. His work further informs of the postmodernist self-effacement of the artist. He engaged in "a purposively modest art which refuses to dissolve its distinctive components into a signature look."[17] Downes himself contributed to the literature of postmodernism. He saw in postmod-

Rackstraw Downes, *The Tennis Courts in Riverside Park at 119th Street* (1978–80). Oil on canvas, 18 ¾ × 46 ¼". *Collections of Whitney Museum of American Art. Purchased with funds from the Louis and Bessie Adler Foundation, Inc., Seymour M. Klein, President.*

ernism the opportunity to pick up where landscapist John Constable had left off in the nineteenth century, to recover the "presentness" of experience, of real places, in preference for formal considerations.

Photo-Realism was heavily representational, but it also allowed for artistic creativity. Audrey Flack pioneered photo-Realism with her "Kennedy Motorcade" in 1964. She, too, after her studies at Yale, became involved in abstract expressionism and she carried into realism a particular interest in the rearrangement of forms. Furthermore, Flack was a self-consciously female artist in a genre dominated by men. Louis Meisel wrote: "Flack has painted from a female point of view. It is hard to know if she is interpreting the world as a woman or is intentionally politicizing. Suffice it to say that her vision is totally different from that of the other major Photo-Realists, all of whom are men."[18] Flack's "Vanitas" paintings accentuate postmodernist themes of stylistic intermixtures, temporal fragmentation, and symbols of chance and fate.

For the most part, the Super Realists themselves reinforced their reputed conservatism. Robert Bechtle disavowed any social commentary in his art. He said of his work, "there is a realization that my roots are there. It deals with a very middle-class life-style which I tried to get away from when I was younger. But eventually I had to admit to myself that was who I was, and, like it or not, had to deal with it."[19] Don Eddy, who did some stunning compositions of automobile fronts and store windows, said "You can't leave your own world. You're born into it."[20] Robert Cottingham remarked: "I hate to intellectualize too much about my work. I would rather let the painting do the talking."[21] Bechtle again: "I am interested in the ordinariness [of things] and in the challenge to make art from commonplace fare."[22] An important shift accompanied these concerns. Postmodernist painting deferred to the viewer. It honored consumption of the art product over concentration on its production, in which authorial priority prevailed. Consider the assertion by modernist painter Mark Rothko: "It is our function as artists to make the spectator see the world our way—not his way."[23] Postmodernist painters made no such demands.

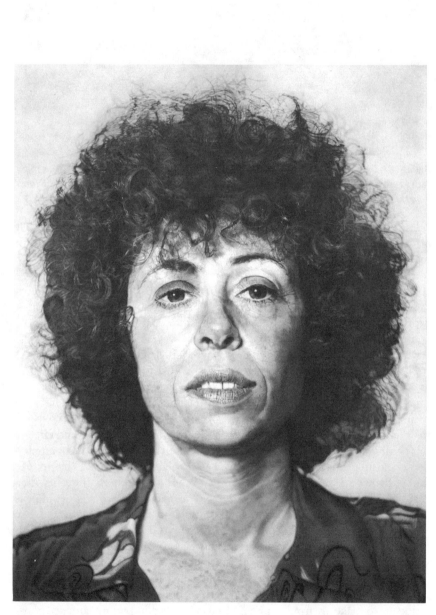

Chuck Close, *Linda* (1975–76) . Acrylic on linen. *Courtesy of the Pace Gallery, New York.*

Pattern painting, or decorative painting, debuted in the mid-1970s. It, too, had to make its way against the prejudices of formalism. "Decorative" art had been disparaged in official art circles for several decades. But this Western prejudice did not apply in other traditional cultures, such as Byzantine or Islamic, from which this genre borrowed heavily. Indeed, pattern painting sought to recover what modernism left out, including non-Western traditional folk elements and domestic crafts such as hooking, sewing, and quilting.[24] "P and D," under the initiative of Robert Zakanitch in his New York studio in 1974, became a movement to restore the decorative to primacy in art. Pattern painters produced large, boldly colored paintings or sewed works that resembled wallpaper designs, particularly floral patterns; or, as in the example of Joyce Kozloff, they made paintings that looked like quilts or rugs. Rich and luxuriant and by no means unsophisticated, pattern painting struck against the puritanism of modernism, particularly the austerity of minimalism.[25] Renowned artist Frank Stella, who began his career in minimalism, moved into pattern painting at this time.[26]

Pattern painting has been called "one of the most important developments of American art during the 1970s."[27] Despite its detractors, who dismissed it as trivial or associated it with commercialism, pattern painting won support from critics looking for a more inclusive art program for the United States. They joined it to the reformist political agenda of the 1970s. Artist/critic John Perreault, who had joined in political causes with other artists, welcomed decorative arts' opening to Third World cultures. These more traditional cultures, he believed, helped undermine Western scientism and rationalism, often associated by the Left with the technocratically oppressive societies of advanced industrial civilizations. Perreault saluted the inspirations from Islamic, Far Eastern, Celtic, and American Indian sources that informed the new decorative styles.[28]

Pattern painting also became allied with the new feminist movement in American art. Traditional antifemale prejudices, some argued, explained the longstanding disparagement of decorative elements in art and crafts. Pattern art now sought to recover these "feminine" forms. Besides Kozloff, who contributed to abstract pattern painting, Cynthia Carlson offered painterly styles, and Valerie Jaudon non-painterly subjects. Major leaders in the feminist art movement, Miriam Schapiro and Judy Chicago, also made commitments to pattern painting. Schapiro, an important theorist of feminist art, looked for the images and forms of female art that gave it particular definition.[29]

The 1970s began with radical hopes in art. By decade's end, it seemed that the American art world had lapsed back into conformity and loss of critical nerve. The "political" question of art fascinated critics in this decade as it in turn induced some of their strongest polemical writings and harshest judgments. This chapter will first examine the activities of artists who took up protest and joined their work in art to a larger political agenda. Later it will

Valerie Jaudon, *Rosedale* (1976). Oil and wax on canvas, 72 × 72". *Courtesy of Sidney Janis Gallery, New York.*

explore the fate of the avant-garde in the 1970s and what it signified for American society and politics.

From late January to early February in 1967 some six hundred artists calling themselves Angry Artists Against the War in Vietnam organized protest activities in New York City. Productions included painting and sculpture, poetry, theater, film, and a variety of performances and "happenings." A 10' high and 120' long *Collage of Indignation* appeared in the Loeb Student Gallery of New York University, a centerpiece of the demonstration and the collaborative effort of some 150 painters and sculptors.[30]

In 1968 the Art Workers Coalition formed a protest against the Museum of Modern Art. The narrow issue was MoMA's exhibition on Dadaism. The protesting artists took offense at the art establishment's display of what they considered "an anarchistic and revolutionary movement"—Dadaism—and could see in its action a familiar effort to co-opt and neutralize avant-garde art. More dramatically, the next year the sculptor Takis removed his piece from the MoMA display room. He issued a statement that said, "the time has come to demystify the elite of the art rulers, directors of museums, and trustees."[31]

Takis's pronunciation spoke directly to the larger question of museums' roles in the art world, a highly political matter in this decade. Carl Andre participated actively with the anti-Vietnam War artists, directly joining the war to his paintings. He also became the major voice of criticism against the "Art Establishment"—the art museums and their commercial affiliates, the art galleries. Using a New Left standard, Andre contended that museums played the major role in turning art products into commodities. "Once a work has been shown in a gallery or museum," he said," it has a quality that was conveyed to the work by the splendor of the museum or the prestige of the gallery. What the museum is really interested in is not quality but commodity—Ma Bell's princess telephone or Carl Andre's sculpture are now in the permanent collection of the Museum of Modern Art because they have reached the level of commodity."[32] Andre's words, from a 1970s interview, reverberated with 1960s clichés. The immediate problem, he insisted, was "the dictatorship of the bourgeoisie." The museum boards, he said, "are the very corporate leaders and bankers who dominate the class system in America and whose interests directly oppose those of workers and artists."[33] Art critic and editor Gregory Battock put it most forcefully:

> The trustees of the museums direct NBC and CBS, *The New York Times,* and the Associated Press, and that greatest cultural travesty of modern times—the Lincoln Center. They own A.T.& T., Ford, General Motors, the great multi-billion dollar foundations, Columbia University, Alcoa, Minnesota Mining, United Fruit, and AMK, besides sitting on the boards of each other's museums. The implication of these facts are enormous. Do you realize that it is those art-loving, culturally committed trustees of the Metropolitan and Modern museums who are waging the war in Vietnam?[34]

To many observers it seemed that early 1970s art reflected reformist political causes. Whether there was more hope than reality in this concern is another question. Already conventional wisdom was asserting that the avant-garde was dead, that the great hopes of the modernist movement and its challenge of a new consciousness lay suspended on the walls of the establishment museums or dormant on suburban living-room coffee tables. Nonetheless, the art scene was an expansive one. In his book *The Object of Performance,* a study of the avant-garde in the 1970s and 1980s, Henry M. Sayre found that a self-conscious avant-garde movement, deliberately situating itself outside the museums (or otherwise demanding a broadened museum format) came into being in the 1960s and continued thereafter. This "postmodernist" avant-garde, as Sayre called it, opened up the art world to new voices while also resisting the marketplace and bourgeois co-optation. Sayre asserted that however much the modernist tradition had succumbed to the commercial establishment, postmodernist, radical art revived a different, antiformalist modernism, as represented by Dadaism and Surrealism, for example. This "other" side of modernism assumed a subversive posture against the reigning social order and the cultural order, too.[35]

The postmodernist avant-garde belonged to the art that went into hiding. One had to look to the Soho district in New York City, for example, to find it. Paula Cooper's gallery opened in 1968, and by the early 1970s the *Gallery Guide* listed dozens more that showed new and experimental art. "Performance art" became a major vehicle of the avant-garde—from San Francisco Be-Ins in 1967 to theater productions such as Robert Wilson's "Einstein" in 1976. As poststructuralist literary criticism signified a concern for what is left out, radical postmodernist art concerned itself with what could not otherwise be represented. As art critic Craig Owens wrote, "it is precisely at the legislative frontier between what can be represented and what cannot that the postmodernist operation is being staged—not in order to transcend representation, but in order to expose that system of power that authorizes certain representations while blocking, prohibiting and invalidating others."[36]

Feminists believed that women's art belonged to the category of excluded representation. Moreover, with the beginnings of the women's movement in the mid-sixties, an avowedly feminist direction in painting followed in the seventies. The first cooperative women's art galleries, AIR and Soho 20, formed in New York City and others followed in San Francisco and Los Angeles. Pressure grew on the art museums to show women's art and they yielded such important showings as *Women Artists, 1550-1950* at the Brooklyn Museum in 1977. Despite the fact that women artists such as Helen Frankenthaler, Grace Hartigen, and Bridget Riley had won substantial reputations for their work, they did not seek to define or produce an art that was distinctively female. The seventies, though, pursued this question forcefully as feminist artists no longer wished to de-gender art merely to compete in the male world. Throughout this decade, critics such as Lucy Lippard and Moira Roth looked for the essential qualities of female creativity, and the various gallery offerings invited speculation about these qualities, too.[37]

Feminism easily allied itself with performance art. It shared with the avant-garde an impatience, or often hostility, toward formalism, judging it to have no political force and no social reference. Performance artists such as Laurie Anderson, Eleanor Antin, and Carole Schneemann gave dramatic renderings that often clearly joined their work to a message of female sexual liberation.[38] Judy Chicago (who had changed her name from Judy Gerowitz) had begun her career in formalist art, including minimalism, as had some of her feminist colleagues. In 1970 she began a feminist art program at Fresno State. She had concluded that her work in formalist art necessarily meant the suppression of her femaleness. Martha Rosler made the same point. She declared the priority of feminist content in painting over formalist considerations at the time that she, too, took on specific political interests. After Chicago's stint at Fresno, she and Miriam Schapiro created and directed the Feminist Art Program at the California Institute of the Arts. There Chicago conceived the idea for her project *The Dinner Party*, a collaborative effort eventually completed in 1979, and judged by one historian as "perhaps the most ambitious political artwork of the '70s." *The Dinner Party* is a triangular arrangement of tables, 45 feet on each side, with table cloths, each differently encoded, and place settings. It cost $250,000 to complete, a measure of the strength of the women's movement and interest in it at the end of the decade. (The project was joined by some male artists.) It combined the major thematic points of seventies art with its emphasis on craft and in its avowedly political statement. On this point, Chicago spoke emphatically: "I am of the opinion that the entire class struggle is based on the division between male and female—and that is what, for *me*, is fundamental."[39]

Greater inclusiveness also meant new attention to black artists. That initiative came from artists in Harlem in the mid-'60s when Romare Bearden founded Spiral, a group of black artists who had come together after the 1963 March on Washington. The Studio Museum gallery at Fifth Avenue and 125th Street opened in 1968, dedicated to showing contemporary black artists. Under the direction of Edward Spriggs, the gallery undertook a national search to identify major African-American artists.[40]

The efforts in Harlem reflected the larger political concerns that had resonated in the politics of the 1960s. They found expression in such movements as the "Black Aesthetic," to be considered in a later chapter. Spriggs wanted to show art that expressed a black aesthetic and argued that such an essentialist quality might be recovered in black painting. Color, he believed, had different connotations for black and white artists. Another spokesman for the gallery, Jeff Donaldson of Howard University, wrote in 1971: "It's *nation time* and we are searching. Our guidelines are our people—the whole family of African people, the African family tree." He would try to have Studio Museum show images to which ordinary African-Americans, without the requisite of formal training, could relate to directly.[41]

In the early 1970s, some in the art community believed that the museums and galleries had simply ignored black artists.[42] But that situation was being remedied just as it was being lamented. Contemporary black artists gained more space in art institutions and significant black artists like the colonial limner Joshua Johnston and the genre and landscape painter Henry O. Tanner enjoyed renewed attention. Nonetheless, the black art movement certainly reflected the radical and separatist ideals of the 1960s. Those artists who wished to promote a black aesthetic also embraced black separatist politics. They worked with black communities in Watts and Harlem and directed their art to the consciousness of an African-American public. As Barbara Rose observed, these artists incorporated neoprimitive and expressionist styles and utilized bold colors and patterning reflective of African textiles. Other social-protest artists used an illustrative and hortatory painting reminiscent of 1930s social realism.[43]

Did art have any role to play in politics and social reform? The question goes back almost as far as art itself, but it had a noticeably dominant place in art criticism of the 1970s. "I myself can't recall a time," wrote critic Douglas

Davis, "when the politics of art were so openly and heatedly discussed."[44] Vietnam, feminism, black protest, and the museum question are only some of the causes that artists themselves took up and to which they made their art a political contribution.

The matter of art's relation to politics was not so easily settled. In fact, the American Left soberly confronted this question, and often with a good deal of skepticism. Many knew that the fate of political art had not previously been a happy one. Others believed political art did not meet any aesthetic standards at all.

One found these reservations everywhere. Artist Abe Ajay had joined the "End Your Silence" artists' protest against the war in Vietnam and insisted that the artist must at every opportunity join the fight against evil where found. But he also urged that "as a strict constructivist, however, I believe that an artist's work should be clean as a hound's tooth of politics and social protest imagery. It is always bad art, sad and dreary and witless. . . .There is no message in the medium."[45] Some of the New York abstract expressionists also endorsed the antiwar movement, but more as citizens than as artists. Adolph Gottlieb in 1971 associated politically charged art with socialist realism and the painful memories of the 1930s. That art he labeled "the worst form of propaganda there is."[46] Robert Motherwell had taken a similar position. "There is a certain kind of art I belong to," he said. "It can no more make a direct political comment than chamber music can." Nonetheless, he fully endorsed artists' participation in art exhibits that joined to social causes.[47]

Great expectations attended the art/politics discussions of the early 1970s. The end of the decade, however, was a scene of postmortems and obituaries. The feeling prevailed in many quarters that American art had abandoned its dissenting role. Some said that postmodernist pluralism had no boldness or definition. They feared that artists had abandoned their segregation from the dominant commercial world and entered into the cash nexus that threatened to define all human relations under late capitalism. Postmodernism seemed to be indiscriminately accepting, tolerant, and playful rather than challenging; passive rather than engaged, at home in the world rather than in contest with it. To Kim Levin, even the recovery of reality seemed like the escape from reality, giving only gloss and ersatz experience of the ordinary.[48] Linda Nochlin observed that the new realism wholly excluded certain subject matter: scenes of work, conditions of social injustice, the poor. "The disillusionment of the late '60s," she wrote, "was transformed into the illusions of the '70s."[49]

Certain conditions underscored these changes. For one, contemporary painting gained a much quicker inclusion in museums and galleries than previously, receiving instant domestication. Second, art acquired a bureaucratic niche in the larger political complex of American government. As never before in the United States it became an object of state sponsorship. It had its own lobbyists importuning Washington decision-makers for financial support to be distributed through the rivulets of federal agencies and state art councils. By decade's end observers spoke, sometimes caustically, of America's "culture industry." And third, while many artists came from commercial backgrounds, many more located themselves in college and university professorships. Art departments on American campuses proliferated. The number of Master of Fine Arts degrees granted by American colleges and universities expanded from 525 in 1950 to 8,708 in 1980. Summarizing these situations, Diana Crane observed that the artistic role ceased to be that of an avant-garde. It lost its alienation from popular culture and middle-class values. Instead, she believed, artists discarded the lifestyle of a traditional bohemianism and assumed a more conventional posture in their daily lives.[50]

Whatever the underlying roots of postmodernism, the conditions of American art at the end of the 1970s induced many expressions of censure. Art, Donald Kuspit wrote, had lost its "critical nerve." Postmodernist pluralism signified to him a bogus creativity, a series of excursions into new (and old) directions that passed for creativity. He did not buy into the deception. Art, he said, had become like capitalism, engaging in production for production's sake. Borrowing from the reflections of Marxist philosopher Walter Benjamin, Kuspit harshly judged the marketplace takeover of the art world. The avant-garde's "mythification of creativity," Kuspit wrote, "compensates for the failure of its radicalism to effect social or revolutionary change. At the same time, compulsive creativity plays directly into the hands of the bourgeois proprietors, for it gives them more products than they know what to do with, except sell for profit."[51] Critical standards in art, Kuspit added, had shifted to an emphasis on taste, erasing any priority of social reference as art's main enterprise. Taste merely served to confuse art with the other products of the economic system, he said. It made art but an ordinary decorative commodity. The art critic, master of "taste," then becomes "the hero of late capitalism."[52]

Critic Suzi Gablik also believed that American art had suffered a loss. She described the antecedent modernist movement in American painting as ideological in character, committed to expressing a truth, however inaccessible the truth might be. Modernism, she added, was dissident and subversive, dissatisfied with the values of the marketplace and intentionally a negative critic of prevailing social practice. But 1970s artists, Gablik believed, had suffered a loss of individuality, and mere "creativity" could not be a useful surrogate. Individualism under late capitalism, she said, had come to mean egoism and self-interest. Art now signified a pleasure pursuit of the purchaser and a comfortable life for the creator, both the triumphs of the West's liberal, materialist ethos. What American art lacked, Gablik insisted, was a "true" avant-garde. The authentic artist, she believed, must "come in contact with the very essence of being." The authentic artist speaks through the experience of alienation; art then becomes a conscious effort to reconstruct the symbolic and cognitive orders of society. By these standards, she believed, the contemporary artist has failed. "He has abdicated the inhospitable role of pariah and now fits into the culture as though he were made for it. Living under the illusion of being an individual, the artist turns into a cog in the bureaucratic machine that increasingly succeeds in controlling people."[53]

Even new art directions of the 1970s that seemed to have some reformist promise were judged for their passivity by decade's end. In an article on pattern painting, a genre earlier hailed for its opening up to women and the Third World, Corinne Robins noted that this emphasis had disappeared. Many decorative artists, she lamented, had settled for "a kind of high fashion Victorian nostalgia" instead. Pattern painting thus joined in the general decline of American art. "In the Seventies," wrote Robins, "we substituted narcissistic self-gratification for ideas, and, indeed, pleasure became art's pose." Art seemed like it simply wanted to "look good," nothing more. The regrettable result, said Robins: "the disintegration or vulgarization . . . of the decorative art movement."[54]

These criticisms occurred within a particular intellectual context. However harshly some commentators judged it, the decade of the seventies assumes significance for its place as the critical juncture in a profound transformation in twentieth-century culture. The great era of modernism was surely ending. Postmodernism was succeeding it. Why, and what did that signify? And what did these terms really mean? The answers to those questions produced an immense body of critical literature, flourishing in the 1970s and proliferating into the 1980s. The 1970s cannot be judged in its full meaning unless seen from the perspective of the much agitated modernism/postmodernism issue. It will be reviewed in this chapter in terms of key aesthetic questions and ultimately in terms of the attending political subthemes.

Modernism in painting, its roots in the late nineteenth century, refers to a tradition begun by artists such as Paul Cézanne, Pablo Picasso, Jóan Miró, Piet Mondrian, Marc Chagall, and Henri Matisse. Modernism came slowly to the United States. A campaign on its behalf, led by the radical group of New York intellectuals associated with *Partisan Review* in the late 1930s, had joined modernism, with its promise of a new consciousness, to a Marxist reform program, the assault on bourgeois and philistine America. When Paris fell to the Nazis in 1940, moreover, the United States was positioned for international influence in culture, enhanced all the more, of course, by its ascendant economic and political position at war's end. New York City suddenly assumed that leadership role for the United States. It received artist exiles from Europe—Mondrian, Chagall, Marcel Duchamp, Max Ernst, and André Breton among them. Furthermore, a group of New York artists, many of them sons of immigrants, took European modernism in a new direction. Abstract expressionism became the United States' signature contribution to the art world. In painting, it effectively conveyed what critics meant when they spoke of the modernist movement in American art.

The New York painters like Mark Rothko and Adolf Gottlieb looked for new directions in painting, wishing to break away from European Cubism and American scene paintings. Native-born artist Jackson Pollack, famous for his dramatic drip paintings, joined that interest. The main feature of abstract expressionism was its nonrepresentational character, with which Wassily Kandinsky had previously experimented. Art now meant a concern with its own forms, hence abstract expressionism's intense "formalist" character. Clement Greenberg, whose famous *Partisan Review* essay of 1939 had celebrated modernism against the dominant "kitsch" of American popular culture, became the major champion of the New York artists. Greenberg stressed the "two-dimensional" standard, or "flatness," of modernist painting and celebrated the "excitement" in formalist art made by "its pure preoccupation with the invention and arrangement of spaces, surfaces, shapes, colors, etc., to the exclusion of whatever else is not necessarily implicated in these factors." This formalist concern constituted for him the work of an authentic avant-garde; anything else was popular, commercial, ersatz.[55]

Some of the New Yorkers set up their own informal art school. They encouraged students to move in their painting from inner feeling to outward expression without the intermediary of a literal object. Formalism, at least in abstract expressionism, became highly subjective art. One of the New Yorkers wrote: "An artist makes lines and forms to satisfy feelings within himself that are not expressible in any other way, the highest things he knows within himself. He writes his own transcendental language."[56] Rothko likened his feelings while painting to a "religious experience."[57] Critic Harold Rosenberg had called the New Yorkers "action painters," a label that stuck. In their own descriptions these modernists amplified that term. "Whereas certain people start with a recollection or an experience and paint that experience," wrote Gottlieb, "to some of us the act of doing it becomes the experience."[58]

To some Marxist critics, abstract expressionism represented a despairing attitude. Artists, they believed, retreated from the anticommunist, conservative mood of the postwar period and from the failed promise of communism as represented by oppressive Stalinism. Now, these critics argued, the ideal of an art unconnected to politics and exempt from the ideological warfare of the day gained in appeal.[59]

In the art criticism of Greenberg, formalist theory became a reigning orthodoxy through the 1950s. Greenberg championed the abstract expressionists as the quintessential modernists and for a while modernist art enjoyed an association with left political hopes in America. But that association weakened in post-World War II United States. Modernist painting acquired a domesticated status in suburban living rooms and corporate headquarters. By the middle 1960s, at least, critics on the Left had largely abandoned their hopes for the revolutionary uses of modernism. They now found it comfortably absorbed into the commodity culture of bourgeois society. Modern art, these critics said, had been neutered by its museum and gallery locations, its bold-ness reduced to the decorative effects and embellishments by which capital-ism had always preserved its legitimacy. Nothing seemed to show that condi-tion better than the cultural glitter of the Kennedy White House. Now the aesthetics of formalist autonomy and individualism were seen as ideological adjuncts of marketplace capitalism. Modernism, the contention went, had lost its adversary status.[60]

Pop art constitutes the transition from high modernism to the postmod-ernism of the 1970s. In the early sixties, a radical shift in subject matter appeared in the works of some New York artists. They painted the products of America's vast consumer apparatus; they exploited the images of the mass media, including advertising and comic strips. Much of the art captured Hol-lywood culture, with its glitz and its glamorized subjects. Derided at first, pop art nonetheless quickly made its way into acceptance. It enjoyed a dominant status to the end of the decade. But its formidable commercial success did not end with the sixties. Roy Lichtenstein's *Big Painting #6* sold for $75,000 in 1970 and in 1986 an auction at Sotheby's yielded $3.63 million for Jasper Johns' *Out the Window*, the highest price ever paid for a contemporary work of art.[61]

Pop art clearly reflected postmodernist themes. It was bluntly matter-of-fact and representational. It displayed a postmodernist fascination with repli-cation, anticipating the 1970s' concern with imitation and reproduction. It did not convey anxiety or alienation on the part of the artist nor did it invite a crit-ical perspective on the part of the viewer. Pop art mocked the pretensions of formalism. Andy Warhol, for example, disclaimed allegiance to any aesthetic tradition.[62] Lichtenstein parodied and caricatured famous works of mod-ernism, paintings by Mondrian, Claude Monet, Cézanne, and others. Critics therefore decried in pop art its want of lofty intention and lack of imagination. Artist and critic Sidney Tillim complained in 1963 that pop art signified "the decadence and destitution . . . of modern art."[63]

But the heaviest judgment against pop art concerned its association with American consumer capitalism. Even if one concedes to pop art a posture of parody toward its subjects—the Campbell's soup cans and Brillo pads and the other iconography of the supermarket, the kitchenware and electronic devices—pop art effected a normalizing relation with the social values encoded in it. Amid the traumas of change and the specter of instability, pop art's subjects imposed a mood of order, predictability, and stability, an aura of certainty amid traumatizing flux.[64] Pop assaulted hierarchies and bestowed a democratic acceptability on all things. It normalized consumer culture and validated the consumption claims of capitalist society, its detractors believed.[65]

Two individuals in particular made sustained efforts to delineate the para-meters of modernism and its postmodern descendant. Hilton Kramer served throughout the 1970s as the art news editor of the *New York Times*. He first offered art criticism as a contributor to *Partisan Review* and then had positions with *Art Digest* and *Arts Magazine*. In 1982 Kramer became editor of the neo-conservative journal of culture, *The New Criterion*. By that time his name had become synonymous with the assault on postmodernist art. He figured prominently in the political disputes surrounding that subject.

Kramer believed that the postmodern era had deprived the art world of high aesthetic standards and had plunged it into confusion. Collectively, his critical pieces focused on one particular theme. The demise of modernism, he thought, had prepared the way for a rash of experimental ventures (that much was owed to the spirit of modernism itself). The art world, Kramer regretted, had become an open highway, with many a vagabond traveller and peddler roaming its way. The United States in the 1960s had succumbed to an antielit-ist mood that disparaged all authority and disdained established standards, as the Left critique of museums confirmed. Kramer complained when museums opened their halls to all varieties of art and made patronizing overtures to the excluded. When New York's Metropolitan Museum of Art offered its exhibi-tion of black art, *Harlem on My Mind*, Kramer considered it a betrayal of stan-dards. MoMA's new director in 1970 opined that "I happen to believe that everybody is an artist." Kramer recoiled from so vacuous a pronunciation.[66]

Kramer allied himself decidedly with the tradition of modernist painting culminating in the New York School. He considered Clement Greenberg "the finest critic of his day," and endorsed his aesthetic formalism. But Kramer, a political conservative, had to face the problem of Greenberg's alliance of mod-ernism with Marxism and the intentions of the New York critics to link the modernist aesthetic to radical politics. Kramer, who never missed an opportu-nity to denounce 1960s radicalism, needed to take up afresh the whole ques-tion of the avant-garde and its relation to the larger society. He made that effort in his important essay of 1972, "The Age of the Avant-Garde?"

Both Marxists and neoconservatives recognized modernism's deflated state, its loss of oppositional power, in the 1970s. To Marxists that state signified a familiar theme—the co-optative power of capitalism, its ability to absorb and domesticate all forces of negation, all principles of opposition. For Kramer, however, the matter could not be described quite so simply. He considered the avant-garde a vital correlation of bourgeois society itself. However much the avant-garde artists judged themselves a critical force against bourgeois cul-tural norms, they actually enjoyed a symbiotic relationship to that culture, Kramer believed. For bourgeois society, he said, was actually the first expres-sion of modernism. With its apparatus of industrial machinery and technol-ogy, it registered a revolutionary impact in all categories of life. Politically, too, the advancement of the bourgeoisie induced the growth of liberal democratic governments, equally revolutionary in their consequences for the prevailing political order. The bourgeois ascendancy, rooted in a transforming capital-ism, produced an ethos of liberation, Kramer wrote, a progressive ideology of openness, newness, antitraditionalism, and expansiveness. That unsettling effect coexisted with the bourgeois ethic's morally reactionary "puritan" side.

Kramer considered modernism the psychic equivalent of the bourgeois revolution, drawing on its economic and political energy and dynamism at the same time it sought liberation from its cultural constraints and moral codes.[67]

At the same time, Kramer argued, modernism perpetuated a specific art tradition, one that each successive generation of artists sought to emulate and expand, to redefine and take in new directions. Every great artist, Kramer said, self-consciously built on his predecessors. However bold and innovative, however hostile to dominant social norms, modernism was withal conservative with respect to a sustaining, great tradition of high art.[68]

Ultimately, then, Kramer understood modernism as a movement that gave visual expression of the dynamism, power, and innovative spirit of capitalism, registering its social, economic, and political effects. It seized on that spirit, in turn, to make a vital critique of those effects, turning against crucial aspects of bourgeois society itself. But bourgeois society, in a manner without precedent, said Kramer, accommodated itself to every challenge the avant-garde could mount. It did so even to the point that the avant-garde assumed a dominant status within bourgeois culture itself. Increasingly, then, capitalist society, Kramer asserted, selectively created institutions—art museums, exhibitions, schools, publications, foundations—that actually served as agencies of a licensed opposition in its own domain. The avant-garde and capitalist society needed each other. When the twentieth-century totalitarian governments of both the Right and Left annihilated bourgeois liberalism, modernism and the avant-garde also met a brutal repression.[69]

But if modernism's absorption into the dominant society transformed the avant-garde, it also changed the host culture, too. Here Kramer and the Marxists saw things quite differently. In Kramer's view, the bourgeois spirit that had nourished modernism was now itself exhausted, "supine and demoralized." It had succumbed completely to its own licensed opposition, yielding all power of resistance to the assaults against it. Herein lay for Kramer the significance of the postmodern agenda. Postmodernism signified for him not only the loss of critical standards in art, but an antielitism that conveyed a new political assault from the Left. Art, he believed, now yielded to the political, and Kramer decried the postmodernist opening to the various forms of feminist art, black art, and issues-oriented art of any kind.[70]

But Kramer also inveighed against the revisionist exhibitions that now flourished in the museums. Kramer defended the role of museums as trustees of the high tradition of art, and saw that trust unhappily abandoned in the 1970s. With the death of modernism, Kramer believed, art had lost the high formalist standards of the great tradition. Museums now felt free to roam the past and revisit long-discredited genres. They felt no constraint, either, in opening to racial and sexual interest groups. There remained only art as politics and art as kitsch. Postmodernism signified the "revenge of the philistines."[71]

Daniel Bell, on the other hand, did not stand at ease with modernism. Bell published his book *The Cultural Contradictions of Capitalism* in 1976, describing it as a sequel to *The Coming of Postindustrial Society*. *Cultural Contradictions* represented Bell's efforts to understand modern culture in terms of the significant economic changes occurring in the advent of postindustrialism. His book provided a long overview, for the situation in the 1970s, he believed, represented a culminating point to an era that dated back to the Renaissance. We have reached the end of the bourgeois era, Bell asserted, and the end of modernism, the dominant economic and cultural ideologies of the West to this point.[72]

The West entered the modern era, Bell explained, in the sixteenth century. It established as its new ideal the primacy of individualism, the notion that the individual is an autonomous and self-determining unit that claims a higher ethical priority than the tribe or established social institutions. Two expressions of this ideal came into influence: the bourgeois entrepreneur and the artist. Both signified a restless quest for innovation, the reworking of nature, and the exercise of the untrammeled self. Each in its work would open up the Western world in a radical way.[73]

These two types, however, Bell said, came into conflict, and that fact constitutes the central paradox of Western culture. Each became fearful of the other. The bourgeoisie, however revolutionary in the economic world, became conservative in culture, seeking to impose on society a morality of discipline and self-control and appealing to established social norms. It sought to channel energy and creativity into the production of goods and learned to be wary of intemperate spontaneity and impulse. On the other hand, said Bell, the artist learned contempt for these "repressive" bourgeois values. Reason, utility, and materialism defined a barren culture, a mechanized way of life, a "cruel, implacable regularity," as the poet Baudelaire put it.[74]

Modernism from the time of Baudelaire signified for Bell a break from the idea of a rational cosmos that underscored Western science, technology, and economics. Art also broke from its primary concern with representation. "Modernism," Bell wrote, "is the disruption of *mimesis*. It denies the primacy of an outside reality, as given. It seeks either to rearrange that reality or to retreat to the self's interior, to private experience as the source of its concerns and aesthetic preoccupations." And whereas art in its earlier role invited contemplation, modernism now offered sensation, immediacy, and impact.[75]

For Bell, modernism had an all too easy time of it. For "what is played out in the imagination of the artist," he wrote, "foreshadows, however dimly, the social reality of tomorrow." Modernism flourished within a bourgeois cultural system that was now disintegrating, Bell said. As capitalism proliferated consumerism in abundance, change and newness became society's governing mentality. Capitalism, wrote Bell, produced a psychic instability that fed on instant gratification. The virtues of the proverbial Protestant work ethic eroded. Immediate self-gratification and sensual indulgence became capitalist society's motivating drives.[76] Writing at the end of the decade, Bell added: "The *visible* mark of American culture in the 1970s . . . was hedonism: a more open life-style, an emphasis on self-gratification, a receptivity to experiment in morals, manners, and dress . . . the flaunting of pornography, the growing and open use of drugs."[77]

Modernism, Bell said, thrived on its adversary, or countercultural role. But modernism lay exhausted because its traditional enemy, bourgeois morality, had given up the field. Modernism had no force against which it must sharpen its sword. Bell here described a situation familiar to every neoconservative in the 1970s—the concessions made to the counterculture by the mainline institutions in the United States. Bell cited the media, the universities, the publishing houses, and the advertising industry. All had succumbed to "radical chic," the fashionable display of the symbols of rebellion and protest by the very agencies of the culture under assault. The majority, said Bell, has no intellectually respectable culture of its own—no major novelists, no artists, no painters. Classic bourgeois ideals had dissolved. Bell's question was surely a rhetorical one: "who in the world today, especially in the world of culture," he asked, "defends the bourgeoisie?"[78]

Essayist Tom Wolfe, in a devastatingly satirical essay in 1975, graphically illustrated this strange alliance of middle-class America and its aesthetic rebels. "Today," he wrote, "there is a peculiarly modern reward that the avant-garde artist can give his benefactor: namely, the feeling that he, like his mate the artist, is separate from and aloof from the bourgeoisie, the middle classes . . . the feeling that he is a fellow soldier . . . in the vanguard march through the land of the philistines." Buying modernist paintings wet and warm from the artist's humble loft, Wolfe said, has a special, pleasing effect for the uneasy, affluent burgher. For he thereby announces to the world that he is not a simple-minded Rotarian or middle-class boob. Wolfe described the situation with 1970s specificity. "Avant-garde art, more than any other," he wrote, "takes the Mammon and the Moloch out of money, puts Levis, turtle-necks, muttonchops, and other mantles and laurels of bohemian grace upon it."[79]

As bourgeois culture and cultural modernism presided over each other's demise, postmodernism followed logically and inevitably, Bell believed. Postmodernism, especially in its pop form, represented to Bell the complete disappearance of the former tension between art and society. It reflected a one-dimensional culture of plenty and the singular ethic of the pleasure pursuit, imbibing the iconography of the supermarket and the appliance store, along with the media imagery of Hollywood. Postmodernism, in Bell's judgment, signalled the triumph of hedonism. Modernism, at least, bore an aristocratic spirit, inviting an elite of judgment and taste to join in its subversive enterprise. In postmodernism Bell saw only the triumph of mass culture. Art became theater, happening, performance. "What was once the property of an aristocracy of the spirit is now turned into the democratic property of the mass," Bell said. Modernism in the loft had become postmodernism in the streets.[80]

Art discussion in the 1970s thus brought to a fruition, though by no means a conclusion, the curious history of formalist aesthetics. In the 1930s and 1940s, Greenberg and his colleagues on the Left sponsored modernism as resistance to the commercial culture of capitalist United States. They sought to define and preserve one area of modern life still exempt from the pacifying effects of mass culture and the reactionary political agenda that mass culture supported. As a conservative in the 1970s, Hilton Kramer upheld similar aesthetic standards. For him, however, modernism stood for a fruitful alliance with bourgeois culture. By virtue of its adversarial power, it was the cultural coefficient of a dynamic capitalism. Kramer judged postmodernism to be the death of modernism, the indiscriminate assault on a high, even elite tradition in painting. Postmodernism represented to him the avenue now opened to the political Left. Bell, with many more misgivings about modernism than Kramer, joined in that dissent.

1970s postmodernist art seemed to create only dissatisfied critics. Those on the Left seemed to perceive in it the triumph of a contented middle America, complacent and smug. Postmodernism signified the dissolution of the radical will, the great promise of the decade before. To those on the Right, postmodernism registered the collapse of bourgeois culture, the triumph of an indiscriminate pleasure principle, the democratization of all distinctions and standards, the reign of permissiveness. We shall see that polemics did not abate when the subject turned to architecture.

five
_____

Postmodernism II, Architecture

In early 1970, a British observer remarked that "something curious is happening on the American architectural scene."[1] By the end of the decade, many others were saying that the United States had experienced a period of profound architectural change. Certainly, the city skyline looked a little different. The dominant tall and sleek rectangular edifices, triumphant statements of modernism's great age, now shared urban space with strange hybrids. Architects mixed and mingled styles and decorative devices drawn from eras past. They used buildings less for symbolic statement and more for accommodation to a familiar environment. Nostalgia, in turn, suggested a mood of acceptance and tolerance. Designers felt free to indulge and diversify, to relax and embellish, to enrich the visual environment. The 1970s would make itself one of the most significant decades for architecture in the twentieth century. Architecture, like painting, played postmodern.

Urban architecture also responded to some painful pressures. The economic recession of the middle 1970s, sparked by the jump in oil prices, reduced federal housing subsidies in 1974 and combined with general economic deterioration to push cities like New York, Cleveland, Detroit, and Philadelphia to near bankruptcy. Big-city mayors, who already faced pressing social problems in their budgetary needs, sought increased tax revenue. But that quest only encouraged more white flight to the suburbs. Most cities, therefore, focused on programs of economic growth. That in turn provided another impetus to postmodernist change.

The cities could not reverse regional or national economic trends, but they did attempt to attract businesses and middle-class people downtown. They did so with some success. By the end of the 1970s, old parts of downtown residential areas, with declining property values and an aging population, saw a reversal in both categories. This "gentrification" process sparked the remodeling of old homes and the transformation of old storefronts. Trendy new boutiques and condominiums took their place. Often, too, this metamorphosis included an attempt to recover authenticity, to expose or accentuate the "aura" of the original forms—the brick exterior of the front or the floral embellishments of a decorative interior. To an otherwise rootless "new class" this archeological retreat supplied a special nostalgic gratification. At the same time, it reinforced an emerging postmodernist culture of images and simulacra, a shift of perceptions that drastically abbreviated the temporal continuum of past to present.[2]

Finally, economic and demographic shifts spurred postmodernist change as cities, often in acute competition with each other, rebuilt to accommodate the new urbanites. Most visible in this change was the mall phenomenon. Both commercial and city interests rejected the barrenness of urban renewal modernism and used the mall for a multiplicity of activities. They gave a feeling of "theatrical excitement." Baltimore pioneered the transformation in 1970 with its successful Harbor Place project, an effort that made developer James Rouse a national institution. Splendid downtown projects like Boston's Faneuil Hall and Quincy markets, opened in 1976, revitalized center-city activity. All of it had special postmodernist accents. As one observer has noted, "an architecture of spectacle, with its sense of surface glitter and transitory participatory pleasure, of display and ephemerality, of *jouissance*, became essential to the success of a project of this sort."[3]

To that extent, then, these architectural shifts reflected the poststructuralist intellectual currents of the seventies. And when some architects took note of them, a few radical experiments followed. Observing the literary notion that meaning is always tenable and incomplete, some designers cultivated an unfinished look. They depicted walls as torn and ragged, built jagged-edge furniture, and left floors in a garage state of unfinishedness. Designers who took deconstruction to mean a condition of anarchy created the term "anarchitecture," signifying a dissolution of established architectural canons. Architect Peter Eisenman gave American architecture a postmodernist turn in his application of Ferdinand de Saussure, Michel Foucault, and Jacques Derrida. Postmodernism used "fictional" devices, he said, drawn from the historical narratives it now implanted on the rational structures, the canonical rectilinearity of modernist forms, disrupting and subverting their pretensions to truth.[4]

Postmodernism also re-enacted the culture of semiotics. Modernism had stripped buildings of any codification save that of industrial and mechanical rationality. Many architects in the 1970s wanted to restore to architecture the readability it once exercised. They sought to recover for it a larger signification in the public domain. Buildings, too, could be texts. Such an effort marked some of the major new edifices of postmodernist architecture, as we shall note.[5]

As did painting, architecture displayed some radical dimensions that had political content. The group SITE (Sculpture in the Environment) made the most deliberate efforts to find an architecture with message. Consider its most famous, and to its critics, most outlandish design. In Houston, the Best Products store shows a broken, jagged roof line and a small avalanche of blocks spilling over the entrance marquee. It appears to be the victim of a bombing or the mark of urban rioting. But cars around the building fill a large parking lot and inside Best Products clearly enjoys a brisk trade. The team of artists, led by James Wines and Alison Sky, introduced the building in 1975. They wanted to make a statement about the critical state of urban decay and its anarchic conditions. They likened their creation to street theater, video art, and performance dance. Many critics and "serious" architects denounced SITE, unappreciative of its dark humor or dismissive of its frivolity. But businesspeople knew the value of the unusual. After its first success in Richmond in 1972 and the notoriety of Houston, SITE won design contracts for other nihilist works in Sacramento, Towson, Maryland, Miami, and Milwaukee.[6]

Frank Gehry also practiced the unfinished look in a series of homes he designed in the Los Angeles area. They had portions of walls skewed at odd angles or set precariously on top of one another. He built with plywood, cardboard, and chain-link fencing. Gehry's methods reflected the California throwaway lifestyle turned against itself. Milk crates, leftover pieces of lumber and glass, old-style plumbing fixtures, worn quilts and textiles expressed an ethic of recycling and responsible use. Gehry did for these "junk" materials what Andy Warhol and Claes Oldenburg did for soup cans and toilet seats.[7] His own home, constructed in 1977, won the most attention.

Frank and Berta Gehry purchased a banal-looking, two-story house in Santa Monica. Gehry enlarged it on the side with an angular sleeve of corrugated metal, glass, and exposed wood framing. In one section, the sheath is interrupted by a bay window that seems to have been set askew. That effect reinforced other oddities that give the sense of dislocation to the structure, likening it, in fact, to a stage set. It looked like so much raw carpentry. Reaction began with Gehry's own neighbors, some of whom complained to city hall. But the mayor called the project "a masterpiece," and the home gained widespread attention. It soon came under review by architectural critics in the *New York Times*, *Art in America*, *Time*, and *Architectural Record*.[8]

Minimalist efforts, however, no more characterized the 1970s in architecture than they did previous decades. Postmodernism introduced some restraints, but, as Philip Johnson would show, it had its great monuments also. Architecture, as we have noted, also confronted some profound and seemingly intractable social problems—the problems of American cities. The violent urban riots of the 1960s revealed what should have been understood by that time: the painful fact that the cities were in states of precipitous decline. Poor housing stock and falling real estate values, culminating in a diminishing tax base for urban governments, defined the financial crisis. A population sunk in poverty, surrounded by crime, mostly black, poorly educated and untrained for useful work, or self-destructed by drugs, described the human problem. In the 1970s, sociologists began to employ the ominous term "underclass" to reference a human element beyond the redemptory efforts of social welfare programs, reeducation, or rehabilitation of any kind. Statistics conveyed the unhappy demographic effects as suburbs proliferated, fueling the phenomenon of "urban sprawl," and draining cities of their most talented and affluent personnel.

In many ways, architecture precipitated the urban crisis. Huge megastructures continued to arise amid the declining neighborhoods that surrounded them, drawing in commuters by day, dismissing them to suburban retreats at night. But the 1970s saw some spectacular, and highly controversial efforts to meet the urban problem. Two in particular exemplify the different approaches taken.

The planning for the Empire State Plaza in Albany, New York, later named for Governor Nelson A. Rockefeller, began in the early 1960s. As one writer has said, it seemed designed for controversy. The work of the firm of Wallace Harrison and Max Abramovitz and built between 1965 and 1979, the Albany Mall, as it became more familiarly known, consisted of ten buildings set on a six-story platform. The ten high-rise structures included four Government Agency Buildings, the Legislative Office Building, and the Justice Building. At the southern end the shorter, horizontally accented Cultural Education Center faced back to the northern anchor, the elegant, nineteenth-century State Capitol. The new buildings stand facing each other astride a series of three reflecting pools and an ornamentally patterned pavement. The platform itself houses a concourse of cafeterias, shops, auditoria, meeting rooms, and a capacious parking lot.[9]

Governor Rockefeller defended the mall as answering the needs for government offices, but also as revitalization for a deteriorating downtown in the state's capital city. The local chapter of the NAACP did not see it that way and charged that politicians had given far less energy to urban renewal than they were giving to this grand gesture. Rockefeller promised to erode the impact of the plaza on its vicinity by constructing a South Mall housing project. It would provide 440 apartment units for lower- and middle-income families. But two years later he announced abandonment of the project, directing the allocated funds for general use by the state's housing authority. Mall construction then proceeded by original plan. Buildings began to open for occupancy in 1971, with official dedication following in 1972. Eleven thousand employees had moved in by early 1974.[10]

Rockefeller Plaza was a testimonial to government. Its conceivers believed that government should have a large visible and physical presence among the people it serves. New York state should have its acropolis, its civil shrine, the focus of the public eye. The idea invited vigorous rebuttal. Paul Goldberger considered it reactionary and outdated, wholly inappropriate for a modern democracy. He considered the mall buildings pompous and banal. Robert Hughes traced the architectural lineage of the mall to totalitarianism and its

Wallace K. Harrison and M. Abramovitz, *Albany Mall* (completed, 1971). *Courtesy of Office of General Services, State of New York.*

representations of power. "One could see any building at the Albany Mall with an eagle on top, or a swastika, or a hammer and sickle," he wrote.[11] Derogatory nicknames of the plaza included "St. Petersburg-on-the-Hudson," "Brasilia in Downtown Albany," and the "Nelson Rockefeller Pyramid."

On the other hand, one could reasonably plead that such efforts as the Albany Mall, if perhaps not the mall itself, spoke to a republican tradition in

America that conveyed ideals of citizenship, of common life in the public forum. They symbolized the transcendent unity among a people of diverse backgrounds and cultures. Noted architect Charles Moore in 1973 found the public realm badly neglected in American architecture. "There have to be buildings that are identifiable as belonging to a lot of people, and used by everyone. [A public building] should not be just a building like a lot of others in a street," he said.[12] Perhaps in our modern age, the older republican simplicity should yield to a bit of the grandiose. Ultimately, the Albany Mall seems in some important ways to have promoted community. It did not bring people back to the city to live, but from the suburbs and the city it drew individuals to concerts and other cultural events. It inspired architectural rehabilitation and brought in some new businesses. Forty thousand people come to the mall on July 4 to celebrate the national holiday.[13]

In the 1970s, no city more vividly symbolized urban decay than Detroit. "Murder City" seemed as much epitaph as nickname. Around the inner city, thousands of apartments and buildings lay abandoned or gutted. Stores and hotels followed the white middle class in its retreat to the suburbs. Detroit led all cities in heroin production and faced a stubborn unemployment rate of around 14 percent. For black teenagers that rate hovered at 40 percent and lives of hopelessness and boredom supplied a growing membership in gangs that terrorized the city.[14] On July 23, 1967, Detroit witnessed the most destructive of the decade's urban upheavals. A police break-in at a popular gathering place of black Detroiters led to rioting in a fourteen-mile section of the inner city. Black and white homes and businesses fell to the flames. Governor George Romney asked for federal troops and eventually 4,700 paratroopers helped quell the riot. The toll counted 43 dead, 7,000 arrested, and 1,300 buildings destroyed.

Many individuals hoped to see Detroit rise from its ashes, but only one, perhaps, had the power to make a realistic try. In November 1971, Henry Ford II, chairman of the Ford Motor Company and grandson of the great hero-car-builder Henry Ford I, announced to the Detroit city council a plan for a massive riverfront project, the Renaissance Center. He expressed his hopes, as this name implied, that the undertaking would launch a revitalization of downtown Detroit. The Ren Center would include a convention-size hotel, business offices, shops, restaurants, and entertainment facilities. Ford also announced the choice of the architect for the project—the singular and legendary John Portman.[15]

Portman's appointment to this ambitious project was news in itself. No other architect of the 1970s made new adventures in design so visible to so many Americans. Born in 1924, Portman grew up in South Carolina and Atlanta, Georgia, where he trained at Georgia Tech University. By the 1970s, he had formed several different companies, all based in Atlanta. That city, too, would become a major locus of the Portman signature. Peachtree Center featured the tall shimmering towers, lined by the interior elevators that rose

John Portman, *Bonaventure Hotel,* Los Angeles (1977). *Courtesy of Michael Portman Photography.*

smoothly and quietly in the middle of the expansive ground floor plazas of these slick and elegant Hyatt-Regency hotels. It featured multistoried atriums with cantilevered balconies and walkways, "lakes," and other emulations of nature. By the middle seventies, Portman's name attached to such mega-enterprises as the Embarcadero Hotel in San Francisco and the Bonaventura Hotel in Los Angeles.[16]

Portman built buildings and also wrote about them. He believed that in every sense he was taking up the cause of the cities, saving them. He addressed the challenge of the suburbs and believed that the cities could meet it only by remaking themselves as cultural and social centers. He spoke, therefore, of the "coordinate unit," a facsimile village where everything lies within reach of the pedestrian. "There must be a total life involvement," he said, and not in any mundane fashion. He wanted buildings to "enliven the human spirit." He wanted cities to give their walkers "a sense of eager expectancy, sure that around the next corner there will be a different vista, a change in pattern, texture, mood or sound." Like the founding modernists, Portman assigned to architecture a reforming role, but a meliorative, not a utopian one. Portman wanted architects to be "master coordinators of cities."[17] They must anticipate the future by understanding real estate values and growth patterns, market conditions and financial climates. Portman himself typified a new breed of architects who exercised considerable influence in urban planning.

In 1977, the Detroit Renaissance project boasted one superlative at least— the most expensive architectural project in American history. And all of its $377 million price tag came from private money. Ford's financial colleagues elicited the involvement of fifty-one major corporations, each with a substantial stake in the city of Detroit. They included General Motors, Chrysler, B. F. Goodrich, Firestone, Bendix, and Gulf & Western. Portman's design prescribed a 73-story reflecting glass hotel, putatively the tallest in the world, and a half dozen lower buildings in geometric modernist form. Enclosed walkways and a four-story pedestrian mall of housing shops and restaurants interconnected the structure.[18] The look and feel of Ren Center conveyed every bit a fortress mentality, the heavy, gray walls of the interior inducing a protective barrier against the unstable world outside. Nonetheless, Ren Center was meant to make a statement. Robert McCabe, president of Detroit Renaissance described the product as "J.C." architecture; people were to look at Ren Center and say "Jesus Christ!"[19]

In fact, however, different exclamations flew in the face of Portman's monolith on the Detroit River. Many considered the complex a pretentious and arrogant affront. Goldberger faulted the buildings for their isolation and island segregation from the rest of the city. A *Newsweek* critic likened Ren Center to a "snobby rich kid shying away from lower class neighbors."[20] Others believed that the new complex would seriously harm its surroundings, that in fact Ren Center really showed only disdain or contempt for urban life. It turned its massive walls to the sidewalks on which it stood, allowing entrance only through a few elegant passageways. Against the variety and surprise of city life, it imposed a controlled environment. And, critics said, it sucked the financial blood from the shops outside that give the city its color and interest. "Gone is the beebop and diddy-wah from the record stores," wrote one critic, "the fragrance of the peanut shop, the harsh colors of the Day-Glo socks hung amid the sundries of no name."[21]

John Portman, *Renaissance Center,* Detroit (completed 1977). *Courtesy of Michael Portman Photography.*

Portman remained untroubled and matter-of-fact in his own defense. If people find a fortress protection in Ren Center and the like, he said, so much the better. He wanted to be realistic. People perceive cities as unsafe places and architects must respond accordingly, he said. Besides, people also have a good time there. To that extent, Portman won the recognition of fellow architect Philip Johnson. "His analysis of what people want and his ability to get it done," Johnson said, "are second to none."[22]

And so it went in Detroit, and elsewhere. Megastructure architecture provided the signal landmarks of major American cities. New York and Chicago continued a battle of firsts. After New York completed the World Trade buildings in 1972, twin exemplifications of modernism, Chicago regained bragging rights when the Sears Tower, begun in 1970, reached its ultimate height of 1,454 feet in 1974. The work of the Skidmore, Owings & Merrill firm, Sears Tower held nearly four and a half million square feet of office space in its one hundred stories and could accommodate sixteen thousand workers, including

John Portman, *Renaissance Center,* Detroit (completed 1977). *Courtesy of Michael Portman Photography.*

the seven thousand of the giant merchandiser. To be sure, economic factors, above all the soaring real estate values that compelled the upward reach, partly explained the megastructure phenomenon. But something else was occurring as well. The United States was arriving at the culminating and paradoxical conclusion to the long history of modernism, a curious story in the culture of the twentieth century.

To an observer of American cities in the 1970s, the tall and shimmering edifices that bore the names or logos of America's large capitalist enterprises would wholly belie the intellectual origins of modernism. Its inspiration came from pre-World War I Europe, where, in Germany especially, some architects wanted to rethink the whole function of their profession. Many of them gave primary attention to workers' housing. With a crusading optimism and a zeal that variously expressed utopian and vague socialist hopes, the architects wanted a redesign program that would inspire social change. They issued a series of manifestoes in the decades after the war. Thus, in 1919, Walter Gropius, Bruno Taut, and Adolph Bene voiced the religious or spiritual hopes they held for architecture. They judged its contemporary forms harshly. "What is architecture?" they asked. "The crystalline expression of man's noblest thought, his ardour, his humanity, his faith, his religion. That is what it once *was*! But who of those living in our age that is cursed with practicality still comprehends its all-embracing, soul-giving nature?"[23]

Gropius, with Ludwig Mies Van Der Rohe and others, became a major figure of the Bauhaus School and gave modernism its major definitions. Gropius spoke of architecture's prime concern that structures express the unity of art. They should bring into a common activity and purpose the skills of painters, sculptors, and craftsmen who will "know how to design buildings harmoniously in their entirety."[24] Much like the modernist painters who spoke of art in terms of its strictly aesthetic forms, and like the New Critics who spoke of the poem in terms of its aesthetic unity, modernism in architecture honored the harmony and interrelatedness of form appropriate to a specific structure-design. This concern also liberated architecture, the reformers hoped, from the superfluous decorative devices and symbols that embellished bourgeois style, especially that associated with the grandiosity of Beaux-Arts buildings.

The utopian dimension of modernism, soon to be known also as the "International" style, found expression in the early writings and designs of Henri Le Corbusier. Socialist in his sympathies, Le Corbusier looked to the mechanical forms of the industrial age to inspire a rational architecture. He wished to convey purity of form and undo the aberrant irrationalities that distorted architectural purpose in the nineteenth century. Corbusier issued his own manifesto in 1925:

> Geometry is the basis. It is also the material foundation for symbols signifying perfection, the divine. The machine develops out of geometry. Thus the whole of the modern age is made up above all of geometry; it directs its dreams towards the joys of geometry . . . geometry leads them [the modern arts and modern thought] towards a mathematical order, an attitude of mind that is increasingly widespread.[25]

Modernism thus promoted an ethic of timelessness. It sought to express universalist ideals. It abolished history and it ignored context. A building must incorporate the art-as-technology appropriate to itself, the machine aesthetic that would inspire reforms in all levels of modern life.[26] Furthermore, a society moving toward equality called for an architecture of geometry and uniform planes, nothing to suggest the social hierarchy of the bourgeoisie's lavish and offensive ornamentation.[27]

With the rise of the Nazi movement in Germany and with its aversions to all of cultural modernism, Bauhaus architects departed. Many came to the United States. When the Bauhaus closed permanently in 1933, Gropius went to England and then to the United States in 1937. He became chair of the department of architecture at Harvard in 1938, making it a location of European theories. Gropius and his team designed the Graduate Center at Harvard in 1948 and the Pan Am Building in New York in 1958. Mies, too, came to the United States, in 1938. He directed the School of Architecture, Planning, and Design at the Illinois Institute of Technology, where the next year he began plans for the new campus, to become a major expression of architectural modernism in America. His Seagram Building in New York, designed with Philip Johnson and built in 1958, also became an important register of Bauhaus influence.

Bauhaus architecture may have been an exercise in abstract beauty, but its forms became identified with the semiotics of American capitalism. American modernist architecture thus never embraced the egalitarian or utopian ideals of its European inception. Corporate America adopted the "glass boxes" as a way to fix their images in the public eye. American modernism, in a remarkable cultural irony, came to reflect the United States' economic hegemony in the postwar world. The "universal," aesthetic ideals of modernism now signified the American international presence. Michael Sorkin has written: "The period of expansion and corporate wealth of the fifties and sixties demanded a truly imperial building program . . . overweening government buildings, opulent palaces of culture, majestic corporate headquarters in urban and suburban versions, giant retail complexes, [and] vast highway systems."[28]

Lever House in New York, built by the Skidmore firm in 1952, although not the first of the monoliths, became famous as a new design. Soon the Bauhaus proliferated in numbing uniformity—"aloof, anonymous glass boxes," as one historian describes them, their "frigid hauteur" perfectly suiting their corporate clients' posture.[29] To maintain the buildings' perfect symmetry and integrity to the whole, requirements prevented use of any window air conditioners and specified grey draperies to be hung at each window. At the Seagram Building, office occupants had to situate shades totally closed, half open, or completely open—nothing in between.

From the perspective of the late 1970s, the Bauhaus imprint on American building struck one critic as both anomalous and absurd. Tom Wolfe published his withering critique of architectural modernism, *From Bauhaus to Our House*, in 1981, a reflection on the doleful influence of that school to that time. Wolfe glanced at the Avenue of the Americas in New York, with its "row after Mies von der row of glass boxes" and labeled it "Rue de Regret." Wolfe wondered at the mesmerizing appeal of the guru Gropius and of the other "white

Gods" of the Bauhaus. He bristled at the hardened orthodoxy of white color and flat roofs they imposed on their servile practitioners. Wolfe lamented the Bauhaus project to purify the city scene and purge it of those horrible remnants of "expressed architecture"—the bourgeois yen for false fronts overlaid with quoin and groin, capitals and pediments, pilasters and columns, and other pointless gestures—spires, bays, corbels, and what not. And the upshot for America? According to Wolfe, this absurdity:

> The way Americans lived made the rest of mankind stare with envy or disgust but always with awe. In short [the twentieth century] has been America's period of full-blooded, go-to-hell, belly-rubbing wahoo-yahoo youthful rampage—and what architecture has she to show for it? An architecture whose tenets prohibit every manifestation of exuberance, power, empire, grandeur, or even high spirits and playfulness, as the height of bad taste.[30]

Of course, it was not quite that simple. Modernism seldom displayed modesty and its program gave to American architects what Ada Louise Huxtable described as a hero complex, a determination to show the public the true way. The architect sets his buildings in isolation, that they might the better make their individual statements. But Huxtable regretted that this pomposity exacted a price; American architecture had neglected the possibilities for symbolism, sensualness, and decoration she said.[31] Modernism's critics in the 1970s were saying, in short, that its island monuments—these rectangular absolutes—created a cold and inhuman environment. And they often pointed to one dramatic event to make that point.

"Pruitt-Igoe" had become an international name. Built in 1954 in St. Louis, the multistory public housing project, with the modernist staples of unadorned surfaces and flat roofs, had wiped out nearly sixty acres of slums in the city's North Side high-crime area. There it located its rows of new buildings. Named for a black St. Louis war hero and a progressive former Congressmen, and designed by Minoru Yamasaki (who later did the World Trade Center), Pruitt-Igoe towered above the crumbling houses and flats that flanked it. It was patented Corbusier. The complex became a symbol of civic pride and financial ingenuity, providing "decent, safe" homes for ten thousand people in twenty-seven hundred units. But Pruitt-Igoe soon became a living hell. Assaults and rapes occurred near elevators obscured from the main traffic. Plumbing fixtures and similar objects were ripped out and sold to support drug addiction. The exterior revealed windows broken even up to the top floors. Quite simply, people did not feel good about living in the project. On July 15, 1972, tons of dynamite turned Pruitt-Igoe into a heap of rubble, the final solution dictated by a city task force that, in the end, could find no other solution but demolition. Commented Tom Wolfe: "Mankind finally arrives at a workable solution to the problem of public housing."[32]

Pruitt-Igoe marked the last minutes of modernism's hegemony in American architecture. Already, dissenting voices were raising questions about modernism's effects and by the middle 1970s the postmodernist challenge had entered into public discussion. Among its partisans none gained more notoriety than Robert Venturi. His polemical writings invited controversy and in all he did he seemed to relish it. With his wife and architectural partner, Denise Scott Brown, Venturi brought the postmodernist adventure into high relief.

A young professor at Yale in 1967, Venturi took a group of students to Las Vegas to study that city's architecture. Las Vegas—symbol of all that cultural and intellectual America despised about their country. Gambling capital of the nation, desert oasis of self-indulgence and hedonism, escape route for quick marriages and divorces, Las Vegas symbolized that nether world of glitz and sleaze and low taste—democratic culture's worst. But Venturi had serious intentions. He had trained at Princeton and had absorbed the Beaux-Arts influence from his professor, Jean Labatut. From Princeton he had gone to work with Eero Saarinen, then returned to his home city of Philadelphia, where he managed his father's fruit business. His continuing interest in architecture took him on a visit to Rome where he was fascinated, not by the great monuments of that city, but by its pedestrian life—its piazzas and its complex interweaving of great architecture with the common, everyday landscape of the city. He returned to Philadelphia to join the firm of Louis Kahn and aided in Kahn's effort to effect a retreat from the International Style. Shortly thereafter, Venturi took the prestigious Davenport Professorship at Yale. He had met Scott Brown, a young widow, earlier arrived to the United States from South Africa. They married in 1967.[33]

Before the architecture profession heard Venturi's report from Las Vegas, it had heard from him first in his important book of 1966, *Complexity and Contradiction in Architecture*. It became an opening manifesto of postmodernism. By no means an easy book to grasp, *Complexity and Contradiction* nonetheless carried a clear dissent from modernism. Modernism, Venturi believed, focused too much on the aesthetic harmony that it wanted each building to convey. "Architects," wrote Venturi, "can no longer afford to be intimidated by the puritanically moral language of orthodox Modern architecture." He announced his preference for the "hybrid," for the "compromising" as opposed to the "clean," the "distorted" as opposed to the "straightforward," and the "perverse" as opposed to the "impersonal." "Boring" buildings interested him. "Ugly" buildings interested him. "I am for messy vitality," he proclaimed, "over dubious unity." Against Mies' modernist maxim "less is more," Venturi countered "less is a bore."[34]

Venturi wholly dissented from modernism's heroic ambitions. Again he recalled Mies' words on the need for architecture "to create order out of the desperate confusion of our times." Venturi assigned to architecture no such role. Instead, Venturi, who cited the influence of Kahn, wanted to find meaning in those very contradictions, that "messy vitality" that defined modern life. "An artful discord," wrote Venturi, "gives vitality to architecture." How much order to demand, he said, would depend on circumstances, but the designer should not seek to force all of society's contingencies into a brittle reformulation or through a cult of the minimum. The architect, Venturi insisted, is a problem-solver first and cannot separate architecture from the experience of life. His approach, therefore, "will make room for the fragment, for contradiction, for improvisation." Venturi, indeed, would endorse one of postmodernism's favorite words, "pluralism."[35]

Venturi did not consider himself a maverick or an iconoclast. He wanted to restore architecture to its dominant historic tradition. In some lengthy and sometimes technical excursions, Venturi reinvoked a vital mannerist style in architecture that had flourished recurringly from the Hellenistic period in Classical art through the sixteenth century in Italy and in major architects since then, including the recent Le Corbusier. A recovered mannerist tradition, Venturi believed, would induce a healthy reaction against the "banality or prettiness" in current architecture.[36]

Closer to the contemporary context, Venturi acknowledged the influence of pop. This new genre, he said, took common elements and gave them uncommon renderings. It situated them in larger scale or distorted form. Architecture should establish its own kind of continuity, Venturi urged, by this kind of change. Venturi here came pretty close to providing a neat postmodernist formulation:

> Through unconventional organization of conventional parts [the architect] is able to create new meanings within the whole. If he uses convention unconventionally, if he organizes familiar things in an unfamiliar way, he is changing their contexts, and he can use even the cliché to gain a fresh effect. Familiar things seen in an unfamiliar context become perceptually new as well as old.[37]

Critics took exception to what Venturi said, and they did not like what he did any better. Venturi's architectural firm of Venturi and Rauch got little business in the early 1970s, a fact that he resented. Most saw the Venturis as simply theorists, and they did do much lecturing at colleges and professional meetings.[38] But in 1970, Yale University announced a competition for the plan of its new math building. The contest held more than academic interest, for Yale had been the site of several architectural accomplishments and innovations in recent years. Its stand-out buildings included Paul Rudolph's Art and Architecture Building, the Skidmore firm's Beinecke Rare Book Library, Philip Johnson's Kline Biology Tower, and Claes Oldenburg's monument to Pop art, a giant lipstick sculpture set in the courtyard facing the library. When the Venturi entry won the competition, a victory over some four hundred others, an outburst of protest followed.

The Yale review board, in defending its selection, insisted that it did not want a new "monument" at Yale, a major advantage for Venturi's simplistic

Venturi, Scott Brown and Associates, *Yale Mathematics Building*, New Haven (winning design entry, 1970). *Courtesy of Venturi, Scott Brown and Associates.*

design. One of the judges described the winning entry as "absolutely straight-forward, eloquently simple." Another called it "a fresh statement of great hope for an architecture of measure, of selectivity, of passion for the simplest thing, and highly sensitive to the human condition."[39]

Architectural Forum reviewed the events at Yale and displayed the Venturi design plans in the summer of 1970. It received letters berating them. One called Venturi's scheme "a piece of Junk." Another said it was indeed modest, but it had much to be modest about. Another writer faulted Venturi for making no effort to give the building character; it was not enough merely to be simple, the writer said. Still another respondent took a different angle: "I have a lurking suspicion," this writer said, "that Mr. Venturi is putting us all on, and that the gullible, self-consciously academic jury members have been seduced by his casual iconoclastic approach."[40] The Venturis deflected these charges self-effacingly. They would refer to their own designs as "dumb buildings."[41]

Then in 1972, Venturi, in collaboration with Scott Brown and Steven Izenour, dropped a literary bombshell. *Learning From Las Vegas* put into elabo-rate illustration the tenets of the earlier book. This report from the desert stood as the greatest affront against modernism in the 1970s. (A reprinting in 1977 introduced a slightly rewritten and more artistically modest edition). It thoroughly renounced the ideals of "purist architecture" and urged that designers "gain insight from the commonplace." Venturi wanted to recover a folk, or "vernacular," tradition in architecture and believed that Las Vegas showed the way.[42]

Learning From Las Vegas succeeded as a welcome plea for the democratic culture of middle America, even in its garish Las Vegas settings. It struck the architecture profession at a time when modernism still held its orthodox grip in the universities and trades. It indulged in hyperbole. *Learning from Las Vegas* strains in many places to take the democratic norm, in all its coarseness and crudeness, and merge it into a great tradition in art. For example, in a section in which the authors discuss symbols and space, they effect a tour de force by which motel signs and casinos that line Las Vegas's "Strip" rise into high significance. They write:

> But it is the highway signs, through their sculptural forms or pictorial silhouettes, their particular positions in space, their inflected shapes, and their graphic meanings, that identify and unify the megatexture. They make verbal and symbolic connections through space, communicating a complexity of meanings through hundreds of associations in a few seconds from far away. Symbol dominates space. Architecture is not enough. Because the spatial relations are made by symbols more than by forms, architecture in this landscape becomes symbol in space rather than form in space. Architecture defines very little: The big sign and the little building is the rule of Route 66.[43]

Thus, by the enabling practices of the Venturi trio, Las Vegas forms carried on a conversation with the great classical structures of Western architecture. The A&P parking lot takes its place in the evolution of vast space since Versailles, the high-rise Howard Johnson motel recalls Ville Radieuse, and the billboards of Route 66 perform the same formal-spatial function as the columns of the Roman forum. Effective architecture was always but a decorated shed, the authors proclaimed. Its meaning lies in its signs, from the Italian piazza to the hamburger-shaped hamburger stand.[44] Not surprisingly, critics found all this a bit much.

If one could learn from Las Vegas then one could learn from Levittown also. The Venturi group charged right into the prejudices of their critics in speaking for suburbia, too. The group knew the prejudices it confronted. Did not suburbia, after all, denote all that was conformist, materialistic, and smug about America? Suburbia meant split-level ranch houses and "ticky-tacky" vulgarity. The authors, though, found suitable symbolism in those things. They stood at ease among suburbia's iconography—sculptural jockeys, carriage lamps, wagon wheels, fancy house numbers, fragments of split-rail fences, and mail boxes on erect chains. They all served a spatial as well as symbolic role, and served it well. Yes, Main Street was almost all right.[45]

By 1971, the Venturis had become "perhaps the most controversial figures in American architecture today."[46] But their views were winning approval, especially among some younger architects, to whom, as the *IAA Journal* noted,

Venturi had become "a cultural hero."[47] On the other hand, the Venturis' defense of "ordinary and ugly" buildings, their ease and comfort with the architectural trappings of middle America, associated them with conservative politics. The Venturis noted with amusement that they had been labeled "Nixonites" and "Reaganites."[48] Critic Peter Blake charged that Venturi was "reinforcing [President] Nixon's status quo."[49]

Scott Brown, for her part, turned the criticism back on to the critics. She defined the architectural problem in terms of the unyielding prejudices of the "elite." Its disdain for popular culture perpetuated the sterility of modernism, she said. "We're trying to make [popular culture] acceptable to an elitist sub-culture," she said, so that the vernacular could influence and inspire high culture.[50] As typical of elite, liberal opinion, Scott Brown cited the commentary of Harvard professor John Kenneth Galbraith. Galbraith, she stated, had referred to the common gasoline service station as "the most repellent piece of architecture of the past two thousand years." He wanted strict design controls placed on its like by local review boards. Such disdain for commonplace things represented to Brown the arrogance of the "elderly architectural radicals" who dominated the various fine arts commissions, planning and development agencies, and the bureaucratic rivulets of the Department of Housing and Urban Development, which both Scott Brown and Venturi vilified. Behind this contempt for Main Street America, she charged, lurked the policy initiatives that wiped out old and colorful neighborhoods in the name of renewal. Scott Brown pulled no punches. "There seems to be a very fine line between liberalism and class snobbery," she charged.[51] That charge expressed typical neoconservative antielitism.

Venturi's guerrilla warfare against modernism agitated the architecture profession in the early seventies. Then in 1978 came Philip Johnson's post-modernist bombshell—the design plan by Johnson and John Burgee for the AT&T building in New York. Johnson's career to date had hardly been predictable, but he had been a champion of modernism since the 1930s. So his AT&T design seemed a dramatic reversal. He had received a degree in the classics from Harvard in 1927, and then as an art critic had spread the gospel of modernism and the aesthetics of its stark, purist lines. Indeed, Johnson, with Henry-Russell Hitchcock, gave the new program its American label with the publication of their 1932 book, *The International Style*.

Later Johnson became director of the Department of Architecture and Design at the Museum of Modern Art. After taking a professional degree at Harvard, he finally went into practice. A student of Gropius, Johnson followed the modernist protocol. He later recalled with amusement how Gropius insisted that every building must be approached on strictly its own terms. "We didn't care if a church didn't look like a church," he recalled. Johnson designed his own famous "glass house" in Connecticut and with Mies the modernist Seagram Building in New York, and in 1967 he formed his partnership with Burgee. Their stunning project, Penzoil Place in Houston, completed in 1976, showed a departure from modernist standards. Nonetheless, AT&T was news indeed.[52]

In late March 1978, Philip Johnson and John Burgee stood in New York's City Hall to present their design for the new, $100 million headquarters of the world's largest company, American Telegraph and Telephone. The building would arise at Madison Avenue between 55th and 56th streets. Behind them stood the faceless glass box at 250 Broadway that housed many municipal offices. The architects used that building for contrast. Their new design showed a slender, rectangular slab, soaring up from a $100' \times 200'$ base, a sheer vertical rise of 660 feet without setbacks—precisely modernist. But its base presented a massive colonnade, marked by an eighty-foot arch, providing entrance to the building. Inside, a massive lobby, an arcaded plaza lit by oeils-de-boef above the inner arch and in the end walls. At the back, a galleria, its glass roof supported by filigreed metal arches that joined 55th and 56th streets. At the top of the building its pièce-de-résistance—a thirty foot high pediment broken in the center by a circular opening, an orbiculum, that capped the building with an imposing ornamental crown. It looked like the crest of an old grandfather clock or Victorian bedpost. The most controversial part of AT&T, this item gave the building its "Chippendale" nickname.

AT&T recalled an era when skyscrapers had a base, a shaft, and a capital. The architects said that their design answered their clients' request to give them anything so long as it did not have a flat roof. With this allowance, they designed to make a point. At the unveiling, Johnson and Burgee said they were eager to bring some romance to the city. They wanted a clear departure from the boxes that had come to dominate the city skyline.[53] Simple in sentiment, these intentions, however, provoked vigorous dissent.

By the time of its actual completion in 1984, AT&T seemed a modest contribution to postmodernism. But with its historical references, it clearly embraced the postmodernist idiom. As the *Chicago Tribune* noted, "if Mies van der Rohe were alive today, he would regard this building with loathing, because it is the antithesis of everything he believed in."[54] Huxtable considered AT&T a gesture toward Pop art, one that she did not wholly appreciate. She did not take Johnson too seriously and titled her article on AT&T "clever tricks of art."[55] Others feared that Johnson was deadly serious. Goldberger called AT&T "the most provocative and daring—if disconcerting—skyscraper to be proposed for New York City since the Chrysler Building shook up the traditionalists in the 1920s."[56] But preciseness did not come easily to evaluations of AT&T. Postmodernist theorist Charles Jencks stressed the continuity of this structure to modernism's main aspirations[57] and wondered if Johnson's distorted, massive crown might be conveying a satirical comment on postmodernism itself.[58]

Johnson often responded to reactions against him with a postmodernist whimsy of his own. "Here I am, a modern architect," he said, "and look what

Philip Johnson and John Burgee, *AT&T Building* (designed 1978). *Courtesy of AT&T.*

I've done."⁵⁹ But he also spoke about his work and the postmodernist turn. He frankly acknowledged that Americans' feelings about architecture were changing and his were also. "Today," he noted, "we have a different appreciation of nineteenth-century design. We enjoy its mannerism, its picturesqueness, its vision of imperial architecture."⁶⁰ (Indeed a significant event had taken place in November 1975: a major exhibition of Beaux-Arts designs at MoMA). Johnson particularly could lead the transition to postmodernism. However closely associated with Gropius and Mies, he had never identified his work with the grand, reformist ambitions associated with formative modernism. "I don't believe in revolution," he avowed. The essence of architecture was design, he said, not social direction or some intention to promote social good. Architecture aspires to excite, not to improve. Against a background of modernist rationality and seriousness, Johnson dismissed the jibes against his

Chippendale signature by saying, "man can laugh." And he added that he would work for the devil himself if he had a good commission from him.[61]

But Johnson's hymn to postmodernist cool did have some references to social and cultural change in the 1970s. He cited the decline in America's sense of itself, in the post-Vietnam era, as a utopian nation. He cited a new appreciation of pluralism in American life, as witnessed by the success of Alex Haley's book *Roots*. The environmental movement had furthermore taught Americans to think small, he added. And the vogue of Eastern religion signified an escape from rationalism and utility. All these factors, Johnson believed, invited a look to the past, to a new concern with feeling at the expense of reason. "Maybe progress isn't everything," he remarked.[62] Johnson relished the changed feelings and their possibilities for architecture: "It's a great, adventurous pluralistic future," he said.[63]

By the late 1970s, postmodernist architecture was gaining greater visibility. It had deflated the strength of modernist orthodoxy in the professional schools and had encouraged a new vogue, if not yet a dominant one, among urban architects. Goldberger in 1979 could refer to a current fashion for older styles, for mixing and mingling historical forms together in one building. But he also warned that postmodernism in this way was yielding "a lot of rather facile work," a simplistic aping of the past. Goldberger did admit at least one major exception to the trend, however: architect Michael Graves.[64]

Graves had been a professor at Princeton since 1962, enjoying something of a cult status there. Identified with the group celebrated in the *Five Architects* book of 1972, Graves to that point had shown an interest in theory and abstract forms in design. But he moved toward a postmodernist position later and departed more emphatically from modernism. He included among his new concerns an interest in figurative architecture, for which he made a special plea. Buildings, Graves said, have both a "standard" and a "poetic" language. Design, that is, must address its technical imperatives, but it must not neglect "symbol and ritual." Graves also defined these two concerns as architecture's "internal" and "external" languages. Modernism, Graves believed, did embody both concerns, but insofar as it expressed the symbol of the machine it reflected only a utility, the machine itself. Graves wanted buildings' external languages to have figurative, associational, and anthropomorphic attitudes. With no expressiveness, with no meaningful external references, buildings cause social alienation. Herein lay modernism's sad legacy. Architecture must, urged Graves, "re-establish the thematic associations invented by our culture in order to fully allow the culture of architecture to represent the mythic and ritual aspirations of society."[65]

Critic Vincent Scully saw in Graves the most specific contemporary effort to translate semiotics into architectural form, or, better, to create architecture through a semiotic method. His architecture thus more approximated a literary art than any predecessor's. Color, too, contributed to the communication process in Graves' works. He used colors to give a somber and earthy atmosphere to some of his creations. Said Scully: "They are curiously hesitant, soft, and rather sorrowful in character. They help create a feeling of nostalgia, and tend to suggest age and ruin." Graves' buildings often used rustic effects, suggesting a historical depth and evocation quite in contrast to modernism's ahistorical timelessness.[66]

In 1979, the Portland, Oregon Public Buildings Corporation held a design contest for a structure to be located downtown near the City Hall, the Courthouse, and a shopping plaza. The new "Portland Building" was to house city offices and, on the first two floors, provide some publicly accessible space, including retail outlets, an auditorium, a restaurant, and an art gallery. The competition committee consisted of local politicians and business people, and also the architect Philip Johnson. Early the next year, it announced the three final entries, including Michael Graves', recommended in part because it alone met budget specifications. But Graves' shockingly innovative design for the building offended some City Council members who forced a second round of competition between Graves and runner-up Arthur Erickson. In April, the committee pronounced Graves the winner. In doing so, it soon made Portland the site of the most stunning postmodernist building in the United States.[67]

The Portland Building defies easy description. Here is part of David L. Gilbert's narration, from his extended essay on the structure:

> The Portland Building, as completed in October 1982, is tripartite in composition, consisting of a green base which rises in three steps, a mostly cream-colored box-like middle section, and an aqua-colored, square penthouse level crowned with a smaller rectangular structure. The base is covered with colored tile, while elastomeric paint has been used on the remaining wall surfaces and decorative elements. . . . The base is also articulated with square windows that are especially numerous on the Fourth Avenue side of the building where there is a two-story entrance to the parking garage centered in the facade. . . . Running up six or seven stories of glass are twelve concrete strips painted dark red and topped with projecting "capitals," one capital for each set of six pilasters. Above the capitals is a gigantic reddish keystone shape painted on the wall surface.[68]

Swift reaction to the winning design came from the Portland public. Most knew that this building indeed would gain attention, but they welcomed it not the more for that reason. "We may get a paragraph in *Time*," wrote one citizen, "but we're going to also get three pages in *National Lampoon*." Others resented that a government building should now dominate downtown Portland. "Our public officials are not gods," said one. "Why build them a temple?" Among Portland architects a provincial hostility to Graves emerged. One urged the City Council to "send 'Graves' Temple' back to the East Coast." Upon com-

Michael Graves, *The Portland Building*, Oregon (designed 1979). *Photograph: Acme Photo. Courtesy of Michael Graves, Architect.*

pletion, though, the Portland Building won a wider acceptance and among many, even former skeptics, it became an emblem of city pride.[69]

Postmodernist architecture had evolved by the end of the 1970s to its established forms. It became clearly recognizable in new city structures throughout the country in the 1980s. Postmodernism also coincided with a vigorous movement in historic preservation that had both a national bureaucratic force in its National Trust for Historic Preservation and local, often vigilant citizens' groups protective of their communities' vintage monuments. But while postmodernism flourished with appropriations from the past, one could wonder whether it contributed to continuity and roots, or whether it enhanced the confusion of time in postindustrial America. Postmodernism flattened out the temporal plane. It gave itself the liberty to draw from a history that became a smorgasbord, and historical confusion could result as easily as historical reconnection. In this way, for all its problematical appropriateness, postmodernism in architecture provides a key to the 1970s. It registered the temporal uncertainty and ambiguity wrought by postindustrial change. But it registered also the dialectical operations at work within that shift. Postmodernism dismantled the abstract and universal principles of modernism, but it also refused static replication. It made its appropriations of the past at once whimsical, capricious, and playful.

six

Writing Feminist

The 1970s won the label "decade of the woman." Certainly no movement had more profound consequences for Americans than the women's movement that flourished in the 1970s. From the board room to the bedroom, the redefinition of gender roles and the cultural reconstruction of sexual stereotypes had implications and effects of greatest significance. Like all movements, this one met resistance, but as in 1950 none could have predicted how much American law and politics would change the status of black people in the United States, so did the women's movement make some surprising reversals of long-established ideas and practices. Few would have thought in 1970 that by decade's end nearly half of the students in American law schools would be female.

In terms of its successes and failures the women's movement, arguably, had a more impressive record in the realm of culture than in politics. With the establishment of the National Organization for Women in 1966 and the National Women's Political Caucus in 1971, an expansive reform agenda emerged for American women. NOW's first president, Betty Friedan, had inspired an awakened consciousness in many American women (mostly white and well-educated) with her powerful book of 1963, *The Feminine Mystique*. As the movement coalesced, it focused on one major political objective in particular, the passage of an Equal Rights Amendment to the Constitution. Although NOW operated on many fronts (it had six hundred chapters and twenty-seven different task forces in operation by 1973), it made this achievement its cause celèbre, and to many it became the great symbol of the women's movement. ERA's ultimate defeat in the early 1980s did represent a loss for the movement, but one perhaps more symbolic than real. From local government to state and national, affirmative action programs and court decisions affecting hiring policies and equal protection of the laws made important changes in the legal status of American females.[1]

The women's movement owed some of its inspiration to the radical causes of the 1960s. But for many women, feminism came from their own personal disappointments with the leftist politics of the 1960s. Many women bore the scars of bad or indifferent treatment from their male colleagues in the various protest movements of that decade; marching with young men to take over a dean's office and then being sent out to get the coffee did not conform to their notions of egalitarian radicalism. The "macho" style and militaristic fashions in vogue among the New Left for a while inspired like postures among some radical females, but many soon perceived in it a too familiar version of traditional male chauvinism. Stokely Carmichael of the Student Nonviolent Coordinating Committee had let it be known that "the only position for women in SNCC is prone."[2] By the early 1970s women's grievances with the Left could be straightforwardly articulated.[3]

The women's movement reinforced the American Left, but both politically and culturally it prepared to move in its own direction. It created its own press, with *Ms.* magazine, appearing in 1972, and gaining wide readership. In academic literature, *Signs*, with its debut in 1976, became immediately prestigious, as did others more closely tied to specific academic specializations.

In addressing the cultural and intellectual history of the women's movement in the 1970s, one does so with a sense of humility. Every aspect of the social sciences and humanities—anthropology, history, sociology, art history, literature—underwent major revisions as the result of a feminist scholarship that challenged traditional methodologies, filled in gaps in the scholarly records, and forced new conclusions that found their way into the classrooms. The resultant publications constitute an enormous record and even a whole book on this subject would have to be highly selective.[4]

This chapter will examine the effort to define the female experience and to establish a feminist theory. Like most movements, whether socialism, Marxism, or conservatism, the feminist movement had protagonists who wanted to ground their cause on a firm intellectual basis. The quest for theory took place on several intellectual fronts, but this chapter will focus on two in particular—literary criticism and history. The literary subject affords particular advantages. First, through literature, women intellectuals sought to challenge the whole cultural tradition of the West, to reveal its masculine prejudices, its misleading and dangerous stereotyping of women, and its complicity in patriarchal domination. Second, in restudying literary history, women sought to locate a parallel female tradition, to recover from its neglect a female subculture, and to extract from that tradition the peculiar essences of a suppressed female nature. Third, American feminists defined their subject in a way that contrasted with French feminists. The juxtaposition brings into relief a particular American idiom. And finally, Americans' quest for a feminist theory through literary criticism informs how difficult and problematic that quest could be. The American literary theorists, we shall see, had to confront the postmodern complex that we have reviewed in previous chapters.[5]

The 1970s movement in feminist criticism began in blockbuster fashion with the publication of Kate Millett's *Sexual Politics* in 1970. A graduate of Oxford, Millett was teaching at Columbia in New York City and active in the civil rights movement in the late 1960s. That participation also instructed her in sexual discrimination. She became aware of the universality of male domination and stressed that theme in her doctoral dissertation, which led to her book.

Millett did with sexual domination what Marxists did with class—she made it the major control base in human society. Culture, in this case literature, formed the superstructure of that base. For Millett, all culture was therefore power and operated within power constructs. All sexual and gender relationships, Millett said, including even sexual intercourse, replicated control systems. Millett wrote that "in the matter of conformity patriarchy is a governing ideology without peer; it is probable that no other system has ever exercised such a complete control over its subjects."[6] From earliest childhood, Millett wrote, culture shapes the individual along strict gender lines, affecting character, temperament, expression, and self-worth. "Every moment of the child's life is a clue to how he or she must think and behave to attain or satisfy the demands which gender places upon one."[7]

Millett's book recounted the misogyny of male writers, examining the words and imagery used to portray sexual activity and exposing its prevailing themes of control and abuse. But she also kept the historical conditions in view, and she conditioned her treatment of D.H. Lawrence, Henry Miller, and Norman Mailer on concurrent social and economic changes that affected women. With its totalistic account of patriarchy, and by its recourse to literature as the graphic essence of that totality, Millett's book gave a feverish spirit to the feminist movement and made literary criticism a vanguard operation in the early efforts.

Sexual Politics defined a major project in feminist criticism—the critique of the established canon of "great" white male writers. Her efforts had many reinforcements, improving in subtlety and sophistication over Millet's blunt frontal assault. But the 1970s moved quickly to another agenda item—the recovery of a female tradition in literature, heretofore ignored for want of interest in its existence or known but discredited for reason of its alleged inferior contributions. Once begun, however, this work of recovery sustained a booming academic enterprise, and it raised some important questions for feminism, too.

Ellen Moers' book of 1976, *Literary Women*, conveyed the enthusiasm of new beginnings. She cast a wide net across England and America to portray a literary procession of women novelists and poets, a whole separate world of letters, but also personal friendships and communications. She described a precise, parallel tradition to male writers. She effectively located her female subjects in the particular circumstances in which they functioned and these descriptions give a rich, empirical texture to her narratives. *Literary Women* broke new ground and generated excitement by its publication.

In light of ensuing developments in feminist scholarship, *Literary Women* acquires a particular significance, though its prominence has faded. Moers, for one, gave an historical overview that showed little interest in trying to define female writing or to explore its special characteristics and aesthetic qualities. She insisted that "there is no single female tradition in literature. . . ."; "there is no such thing as *the* female genius, or *the* female sensibility." Nor was there a female style, as such, in women's literature.[8] Others who followed, though, would seek out more essentialist qualities in their subjects, a mark of the American critical effort in particular.

Nonetheless, Moers contributed to an emerging American theoretical position. She grounded her subject in history and experience, but also located a viable feminine realm in writing. Because that effort came to be questioned, one should note Moers' particular contribution to it. Moers did not seek out a feminine voice, but she successfully marked off the boundaries of a woman's sphere in literature. Consider her remarkable paragraph on the American poet Emily Dickinson:

> The real hidden scandal of Emily Dickinson's life is not the [personal] romances upon which biographers try vainly to speculate, but her embarrassing ignorance of American literature. She knew Emerson's poetry well, and perhaps a little Thoreau and Hawthorne; but she pretended, at least, not to have read a line of Whitman, no Melville, no Holmes, no Poe, no Irving; and none of the colonial New England poets. Instead she read and reread every Anglo-American woman writer of her time: Helen Hunt Jackson and Lydia Maria Child and Harriet Beecher Stowe and Lady Georgina Fullerton and Dinah Maria Craik and Elizabeth Stuart Phelps and Rebecca Harding Davis and Francesca Alexander and Mathilda Mackarness and everything that George Eliot and Mrs. Browning and all the Brontës wrote.[9]

Moers gave the notion of a dualistic tradition in American letters a powerful evocation.

With respect at least to advancing American theory, Elaine Showalter's book of 1977, *A Literature of Their Own*, marked a step forward. Her study examined British women writers from Charlotte Brontë to Doris Lessing and she approached it in a quite self-conscious way. She believed that women writers had at least contemplated whether a persistent female voice in literature might transcend individual identities and experiences and assume a collective form in art. She noted also that, pronunciations to the contrary, this question was by no means new, that "many early interpreters had the indistinct but persistent impression of a unifying voice in women's literature."[10]

As did Moers, Showalter searched for the lost "minor" voices of women's literary past. She wanted to move beyond the select group of "Great Traditionalists"—Jane Austen, the Brontës, George Eliot, Virginia Woolf—who have been permitted membership in the literary elite. For it was these other voices who forged the links from one generation to the next and created a tradition that otherwise had no sustenance. These others also provided essential connections between women's lives and the conditions that defined their legal, social, and economic status. For Showalter wanted emphatically to historicize women's literature. However much she hoped to see a continuing female subject, she did not want to mythologize it. The female voice always sounded through its particular circumstances, the experience of women at a particular time. Showalter recognized though that any rendering of an essentialist female subject played back into the stereotypes that had governed depictions of literary women since the Victorian era.[11]

Nonetheless, the need to define and elucidate a female tradition governed Showalter's concerns. She would avoid abstracting the feminine by rooting it in history, and history in turn would give her subject its ballast and continuity. Showalter knew the careful middle course she had to follow.

> I think that . . . the female literary tradition comes from the still-evolving relationships between women writers and their society. Moreover, the "female imagination" cannot be treated by literary historians as a romantic or Freudian abstraction. It is the product of a delicate network of influences operating in time, and it must be analyzed as it expresses itself, in language and in a fixed arrangement of words on a page, a form that is itself subject to a network of influences and conventions, including the operations of the marketplace.[12]

Showalter here defined a key American emphasis, the positing of a female subject, not as an innate gender essence, but as a particular self-awareness specifically conditioned in time and place.

Finally, Showalter structured her study in a way that illustrated these stages. She described overlapping patterns of historical evolution in her women writers. The first, long period, she said, finds women's writing emulating the prevailing models of the dominant male tradition. It internalizes its aesthetic standards and social norms. The second produces a protest against these standards. It demands equal status for women's writing or even its autonomy. The third phase brings a conscious self-discovery, a turning inward and a search for identity. Showalter labeled these three phases "feminine," "feminist," "female." They often overlapped and sometimes even described the career evolution of an individual woman writer.[13] Ontogeny could recapitulate phylogeny.

With the publication of Sandra M. Gilbert and Susan Gubar's *The Madwoman in the Attic* in 1979, feminist literary history attained another scholarly height. This imposing work, a study of woman writers in the nineteenth and twentieth centuries, advanced American feminist interpretation considerably. Its speculations took on key questions about the nature of the female self and, however much it showed that self to be hidden in double meanings and elusive allegories, its confirmations helped to define the particularly American mode of literary feminism prevalent in the 1970s. But also, this monumental book brought the American effort into a kind of convergence with French feminism and it takes us into an analysis of that important moment of this decade. *Madwoman* introduced a heavy psychoanalytical dimension to literary feminism, it reflected some thematic postmodern tendencies, and it related woman's literature to the special historical circumstances that govern its discourse.

Gilbert and Gubar considered women's writing a problem in power and culture. Like the Western Marxists, they recognized that Western norms have enscribed on writing a hegemonic imprint. Patriarchal linguistic authority excludes women from any authentic place in the cultural tradition, they said. The very word "author" connotes authority, a power to describe and enforce belief and action. Writing conveys notions of a virile, generative force. John Ruskin once referred to the "penetrative imagination" of the writer, "a possession-taking faculty" that pierces to the heart of experience "to throw up what new shoots it will." The poet becomes God the Father, a paternalistic ruler of the fictive world he has created. Thus, Gilbert and Gubar asked the metaphorical question that opened this book and prevailed throughout: "Is a pen a metaphorical penis?"[14]

These considerations inform why, for Gilbert and Gubar, the positing of a female subject, a woman author, is problematic from the outset. For if a profoundly cosmic, masculine Author provides the sole legitimate model of literary creation, if the pen is indeed a metaphorical penis, by what means do females generate texts? The dilemma thickens when patriarchal assumptions also make woman the creation of men, a creature "penned" by men and hence, too, "penned in" by men. Woman as a sentence spoken by male authorship is also "sentenced" to dependent selfhood by men. Gilbert and Gubar here raised questions about language and its gender connotations that French feminists had already undertaken. The two Americans applied them to the critical question about a feminine identity in literature: "Since both patriarchy and its texts subordinate and imprison women, before women can even attempt that pen which is so rigorously kept from them they must escape just those male texts which ... deny them the autonomy to formulate alternatives to the authority that has imprisoned them and kept them from attempting the pen."[15]

Woman as writer then must first come to terms with those images that male artists have created of her sex——the images of angel and monster, saint and seductress, woman both worshipped and idolized, feared and condemned.[16] Virginia Woolf wrote that women must "kill" the "angel in the house" and her necessary opposite, the "monster in the house." As self-defini-tion must precede self-assertion, the assault on the patriarchal norms becomes the bold prerequisite for the female who takes up the pen.

To explain that precarious course, Gilbert and Gubar drew on the model provided by Harold Bloom's influential book of 1975, *The Anxiety of Influence*. As noted in a previous chapter, Bloom studied literature as the critical warfare of fathers and sons, a process that led to revisions and mis-readings as succes-sive male writers struggled to liberate themselves from the dominant presence of predecessors, to overcome, in short, the anxiety created by their influence. The female writer, of course, confronted a double problem, for her struggle is not simply against the precursor, but against the male precursor's reading of woman. This dilemma, Gilbert and Gubar urged, she cannot avoid; there is no other tradition or image available to her, and thus she must ostensibly accept and work within the dominant sexual imagery. But herein for the two authors lie the foundations of the essential female self of woman's writing, born of this common strategical problem. "Indeed, to the extent that it forms one of the unique bonds that link women in what might be called the secret sisterhood of their literary subculture, such anxiety in itself constitutes a cru-cial mark of that subculture."[17]

This realization of selfhood carries a terrible price, and it is won on dubi-ous terms of success. For in comparison to the male encounter with influence, which builds strength through father-son combat, "this female anxiety of authorship is profoundly debilitating." It assumes the character of a disease, a profound disaffection, a distrust. It bears the marks of isolation and alien-ation, of a loneliness that feels like madness. Creating the female subculture required overcoming terrible odds that could not but leave scars. Gilbert and Gubar made epigrammatic significance of Emily Dickinson's line, "infection in the sentence breeds," and found in disease a dominant metaphor in women's writing.[18]

But given these constraints, how did a female literature emerge at all? Gilbert and Gubar insisted that one did emerge and that an identifiable tradi-tion, a "distinctly feminine aspect of [women's] art," has existed for over two centuries. Scholars have failed to notice that tradition, they said, because it worked by special techniques and strategies that have served to obscure it. "The most successful women writers," the authors wrote, "often seemed to have channeled their female concerns into secret or at least obscure corners." They have created submerged meanings often hidden within or behind the more recognizable "public" meanings of their work. Thus, they left the encodings of a suppressed struggle and story of oppression. Women's litera-ture, when deconstructed, unveiled a signifying absent cause, a political unconscious. But to that extent it was also subversive.[19]

Madwoman suggests important poststructuralist themes. The authors locate their female subject not in the literal meanings of their writing, but in obscurer codifications to which they must have recourse. Often the female writer herself must hide a personal identity within the conventional, the socially recognized and approved character that gender culture dictates. Women writers posed the "madwoman," the irrational "crazy" female and against its source, the rational, controlling patriarchal culture. But they made it also the vehicle of a powerful independence and rebellion and a subversion of the patriarchy. For the madwoman also serves as the author's double, "an image of her own anxiety and rage." At the same time, the surrogate identity helps the woman writer overcome her own fragmented self, realizing the whole and authentic self that women-as-other conceals. As Gilbert and Gubar note, "from a female point of view the monster woman is simply a woman who seeks the power of self-articulation."[20] The female word, then, deconstructs the male logos; it destabilizes the governing signifier, the pen(is).

In the latter part of the 1970s, the developing course of American literary feminism encountered a disturbing challenge from French feminism. Quite abruptly, the liberal and humanistic assumptions that underscored American feminism confronted the profound skepticism of the French feminist critics, who brought to feminism a preoccupation with language. Influenced by the writings of Jacques Lacan and Jacques Derrida, French feminist theorists shifted the locus of the gender problem away from the female subject and its assorted meanings and identities and described language itself as the arena of male domination and cultural hegemony. To the French feminists, American literary feminism seemed naive and ultimately ineffective in challenging patriarchy. Indeed, as the French program made its way into the United States after 1975, it forced some important rethinking on the part of the American interpreters. Some wished to strike an accommodation with the French; others took up their challenge and sought to hold their ground and fashion a rebuttal to the French. In all events, there resulted an intriguing cultural exchange, and it demonstrated that finding the theoretical basis for a contemporary feminism was no easy proposition.

The psychoanalytical theorist Lacan significantly influenced poststructuralism in France and became an individual to be reckoned with in the United States in the 1970s and 1980s. Lacan's theories dealt most importantly with the problematics of identity and the recognition of self. Building on Freud's ideas of the Oedipal conflict, Lacan labeled as "the Imaginary" that period in the child's development that corresponds to the pre-Oedipal period. The Imaginary produces in the child no sense of difference, no separation of self and other, no differentiation of infant and mother, only identity and presence. The Oedipal crisis, however, brings the child into the Symbolic Order, which stage coincides with the acquisition of language. The Oedipal also sunders the oneness of mother and child as the father forbids the child reaccess to the mother and the mother's body. The child now enters into this second stage, the Symbolic Order, constituted by the Law of the Father, the authority of the phallus. The Imaginary Order now must be repressed and in that process it reverts to the subconscious; it becomes an absence, the repression of desire. For Lacan, the speaking subject must exist in language, so that to speak is to accept the phallus of sexual and linguistic difference. Language becomes a substitution for the forbidden mother. Indeed, for Lacan the "I am" of the speaking subject is intrinsically the "I am which I am not," for the speaking subject is also a lack and constituted by lack, that is, the separation from the mother and the repressed desire for reunion with her.[21]

Lacanian theory had immediate suggestions for feminists and important implications for woman as writer. As Jane Gallop wrote: "The Lacanian phallus is thus a linguistic concept. Discourse is phallocentric. Therefore, to have the phallus would mean to be at the center of discourse, to generate meaning, to have mastery of language."[22] (Lacan's ideas were extremely complex and, some insisted, utterly confounding.) To be sure, the entry into the Symbolic Order constituted a difficult and troubling process for males. But as constituted by the phallus, the Symbolic Order posed far more sinister consequences for females. For literary feminists, the Symbolic Order, constructed as it was by language, now raised the prospect of a literary tradition wholly dominated by a male signifier. For a woman even to write required her entrance into that Order and ostensibly her control by it. French feminists therefore brought to language as such a profound skepticism that led them to question even the possibility of a female voice or female subject in literature. They understood precisely the meaning of Lacan's own words that "woman does not exist."[23] For woman is the not-man. Traditional humanism therefore stood suspect (a norm of male authority and identity), and all logocentric systems queried for their essentially male linguistic standards. For some French feminists, what alone remained as possibility in the Lacanian construction was a hopeful, often admittedly utopian retreat to the pre-Oedipal state, to the repressed desire, the Mother, and the recovery of a pure feminine voice.

French feminist criticism also gained reinforcement from Derrida. Deconstruction became a strategy as feminists sought to discredit the pretension to authority that marked all texts. A process of dismantling, rupturing, and fragmenting would assist the feminist assault on the male logos. Deconstruction invited a thorough questioning of authority. Furthermore, in its dissolving of all binary oppositions, deconstruction questioned the very legitimacy of the male/female dichotomy and its prevalence in Western culture.[24] The appropriation of deconstructive practices by feminists was, in the judgment of one advocate, "a serious act of insubordination." Textual criticism becomes an effective political tool as "the textual reader joins the ranks of the disloyal and unfaithful."[25]

This discussion of the French reception in the United States will look at that event mostly through the eyes of the American women who helped give it an audience in this country. What did they define as essential in the French writers and what did they select for Americans' considerations? How did they respond?

Elaine Marks commented, with respect to French feminist writings, that they are "impenetrable to the uninitiated and unfamiliar to the American feminist critic who follows the empirical mode."[26] Her point might already have been observed by readers of an essay published the year in which *Signs* made its debut. Publication of Hélène Cixous's "The Laugh of the Medusa," in the first volume of this important American journal of feminist scholarship, signified a new opening to the French. A powerful, turbulent, rhetorically charged essay, it informed how French feminism made language itself the medium of criticism. "The Laugh" did not present a logically argued position. But Cixous's essay was nonetheless thematically French. She insisted that it is impossible to define a feminine practice of writing, for this practice can never be theorized. That does not mean, on the other hand, that a feminist writing does not exist. Woman's writing, she urged, will simply have to surpass the discourse that regulates the phallocentric system and will somehow have to circumvent the male-dominated philosophical-theoretical language. A feminist practice of writing, Cixous urged, "will be conceived of only by subjects who are breakers of automatisms, by peripheral figures that no authority can ever subjugate."[27]

However discursive Cixous's essay was, its forceful points often emerged clearly. Here she makes an emphatic French statement:

> I maintain unequivocally that there is such a thing as *marked* writing; that, until now, far more extensively and repressively than is ever suspected or admitted, writing has been run by a libidinal and cultural—hence political, typically masculine—economy; that this is a locus where the repression of women has been perpetuated, over and over, more or less consciously, and in a manner that's frightening since it's often hidden or adorned with the mystifying charms of fiction; that this locus has grossly exaggerated all the signs of sexual opposition (and not sexual difference), where women has never *her* turn to speak—this being all the more serious and unpardonable in that writing is precisely *the very possibility of change*, the space that can serve as a springboard for subversive thought, the precursory movement of a transformation of social and cultural structures.[28]

Elaine Marks's essay appeared in *Signs* in 1978 and reflected the growing American awareness of the French directions in feminist theory. Marks observed that the Americans and the French pursue their goals differently. The American writers (and this was true even before *Madwoman* was published) looked to history to recover buried and neglected female voices. This reconstruction of the female subject began amid worldly realities of time and place and was accessible through empirical investigation. French feminism never had such an interest in historical recovery and mostly doubted both the success and the usefulness of such acts of recovery. For them, repression connoted something different, and they looked for a female subject buried in the unconscious. Such a recovery would also be immensely difficult and perhaps hopeless, they believed. One would have to find one's way back behind all the surface fortifications established by the phallic logos or otherwise fashion a new disruptive language altogether. In any event, for the French, psychology outweighed history in emphasis.[29]

According to Marks, the French feminist theorists intended something other than the Americans did when they spoke of "difference." Differentiation for the Americanists meant the differences in women's experience. Those differences explained the special characteristics in women's writing, as distinguished from men's. French feminists, on the other hand, drawing on Derrida's meaning of "différance," meant by difference that which has been repressed in the signifying practices peculiar to Western culture. The French thus asserted that women have been invisible, absent, that difference has been repressed and that there has been only one voice, a male voice that women themselves have been compelled to employ. Consequently, when a woman wrote, or sought to speak herself into existence, she was forced to speak in something like a foreign tongue, a language for which she felt ill-fitted. Often the resultant effort suggested idiosyncracy or eccentricity, even madness.[30]

These considerations in turn posed some problems for the French feminists, and one could identify two divergent groups marked by their different responses. One group, represented by Julia Kristeva, focused on what she called "le semiotique," the pre-Oedipal sounds exchanged between mother and child that precede installation of the father's symbolic language. Kristeva, however, did not describe the semiotic as another language or a woman's language. She called it an eruption in writing that disturbs the sentence structure and imposes a dismantling presence from within. Kristeva looked to avant-garde writers (mentioning Mallarmé, Lautréamont, and Joyce) as models. She urged women to seize these models for their own program of subversion. Marks quotes Kristeva: "What we must do is to help women understand that these modern breaks with tradition and the development of new forms of discourse are harmonious with the women's cause. By participation in this activity of subversion (which exists on a linguistic, family, and social level) and in the growth of new epistemes they will be able to see this as well."[31]

Kristeva nonetheless did not want to assign any essentialist qualities to the "feminine." Her point had both intellectual and political significance. "Woman," she said, could not be represented; she "is outside definitions and ideologies." ("*La femme, ce n'est pa ça*" is her oft quoted comment.) The category "women," in short must get beyond the rule of the *Logos*. "Feminism" must not become another "ism" (whether humanism, Marxism, or socialism) within the logocentric system. If it returns to be joined to a binary opposition with "man," it can only perpetuate its marginality and its powerlessness, a separate cultural space, the impotent Other.[32]

For another group of French theorists, however, the necessity of a different woman's language, an *écriture féminine*, governed their critique. Cixous and Luce Irigaray wanted to dismantle the authoritative Logos, with its assumptions of a dominant phallocentric discourse. They wished to "threaten the masculine edifice" with its presumption of an eternal and natural truth. An *écriture féminine*, however nonsensical and irrational it may appear to be, must be invoked, they believed, to question the "objective" and "impersonal" standards of the dominant discourse. For this language, they advised, is ultimately rooted in claims to power and control and related intimately to the repressed condition of women.[33] Cixous stated this point most forcefully: "Everything turns on the Word: everything is the Word and only the Word . . . we must take culture at its word, as it takes us into its word, into its tongue. . . . No political reflection can dispense with reflection on language, with work on language." So if women have been trapped in the symbolic order, they will mark their escape from it by producing texts that re-write it.[34]

As French feminist theory gained in recognition and influence, American literary feminism became identified with certain characteristics that now came under heavy scrutiny. By the end of the 1970s there existed what one might almost call an American feminist canon, consisting of works reviewed above and others that further contributed to an impressively large scholarship. Different focuses and different perspectives prevailed in these works, but nonetheless American feminist scholarship, in literature especially, bore certain eminent traits, or so foreign observers belived. In summary, American feminism was humanistic and bourgeois in character.

From the outset, the American women seemed to have an aversion to psychoanalytic theory, the major domain of the French. That aversion grew from a longstanding suspicion of Freud. Millett's *Sexual Politics* in 1970 included negative assessments of Freud and his influence.[35] (The publication of *Psychoanalysis and Feminism* in 1974 by the British feminist Juliet Mitchell helped correct this situation.) But Millett herself always appeared to partisans of the French to have perpetuated, in the most blatant way, an essentialist rendering of gender, "a monolithic conception of sexuality that renders her impervious to nuances, inconsistencies and ambiguities in the works she examines." Only a deconstructive engagement, it was urged, would enable feminists to explain how the female voice breaks through, even amid the most rigid patriarchal forms. Although Millett had tried boldly to break down male/female dichotomies that underscored prejudice against women, certain readers found her critical positions too sharply drawn, too "black and white."[36]

Showalter, too, came under censure from French partisans. Her search for the strong female subject had led Showalter to fault feminists like Virginia Woolf who dissolved feminine identity into androgyny or otherwise compromised the unity of the female subject. But this stance, Showalter's critics urged, associated her feminism with a central project of Western humanism and liberal, bourgeois individualism. Thus: "What feminists such as Showalter . . . fail to grasp is that the traditional humanism they represent is in effect part of patriarchal ideology. At its centre is the seamlessly unified self—either individual or collective—which is commonly called 'Man.' " This self, the criticism continues, is constructed on the model of the autonomous, powerful phallus, which has banished all conflict, contradiction, or ambiguity. Humanist individualism can only dissolve the feminine or merge it back into itself. For the French, the feminine must go underground, into hiding and disguise, looking for the faults and cracks in the dominant discourse and therein to conduct its subversions.[37]

Finally, even the "sophisticated" readings in Gilbert and Gubar's *Madwoman*, with its double meanings and submerged identities, failed to meet French critical standards. As Toril Moi stated, Gilbert and Gubar were "seductively sophisticated." "But what kind of theory are they really advocating?" Moi asked. And what are the political implications of their theses? Gilbert and Gubar went the wrong way, it was charged, when they postulated a *real* woman hidden behind the surface text, that is, the author's double or real self. This self, always constituted by feminist rage against the patriarchal system, gave a universality to women's writing. Though a disguised surrogate or alter ego, this self is a subject that writes all texts written by women; it is, in short, a transcendental signified, with the texts as signifier. Such a position sat square against cardinal tenets of poststructuralism, the decentered self particularly.[38]

Not only, according to this critique, does this viewpoint make Gilbert and Gubar's mode of interpretation reductive, as much so as simple Marxist base/superstructure, but it plays into a patriarchal norm in which God the Author is the source, origin, and meaning of the text. This metaphor relies on a patriarchal standard in which wholeness is positive, fragmentation negative. But the essence of the phallus is its wholeness, its monolithic character. "The phallus is often conceived of as a whole, unitary and simple form, as opposed to the terrifying chaos of the female genitals," or often as logical (male) reason as opposed to (female) irrationality. For its critics, the key lines in *Madwoman* are those that hint at the possibility that "if we can piece together their fragments the parts will form a whole that tells the story of the career of a single woman artist, a 'mother of us all.' " This quest for the mighty "Ur-Woman" was a somewhat terrifying prospect to the French partisans, the creating of another monolith, another logocentric "ism," another all-dominant and constricting transcendental subject. For to impose such an authority on the text is to limit it, to confine the multiplicity of female voices, to deprive the feminine of its capacity to deconstruct and to wage guerrilla warfare against all systems of authority.[39]

Thus, partisans of French theory faulted American literary feminism for its humanist tendency to contrive a feminist version of truth. But, as one put it, it thereby failed to "heed the radical implications of post-Saussurean linguistics" and its displacement of the "metaphysics of presence" long dominant in Western philosophy. The linguistic feminists doubted the reliability of texts as faithful transmitters of authentic human experience. Texts must be viewed as signifying systems that inscribe ideology and are constitutive of reality, that is, reality as itself a linguistic construct, laden with its "man-centered binary oppositions." This condition mandated just one feminist strategy, these feminists urged. "Only the undermining of such oppositions, the dismantling of the system that sanctions them, can undo the hierarchical opposition between men and women."[40]

The French feminists challenged American feminists. Each group sought to define the true meaning of the female subject, even if the French did so by undermining the feminine as a subject entity. In the 1980s, American thinkers would make some important accommodations to French theory, but in the late 1970s, many held their ground and sought to consolidate the gains they had made by defending the methodologies they had used. Elaine Showalter's essay of 1979 best illustrates that point and clarifies the American position.

In "Towards a Feminist Poetics," Showalter tried to outline the essentials of what she called "gynocriticism." She remained convinced that a distinct women's literary tradition and a female voice existed, one knowable through history, anthropology, and psychology, too. But by 1979, Showalter had to take note of the gains made by French theories that diluted these convictions. She insisted, however, that the new language-based feminism could contribute little to an effective feminism. Much of the appeal of the new methodologies—structuralism, deconstruction, psychoaesthetic, and others—she believed, lay in their pretensions to be "scientific," that is "as manly and aggressive as nuclear physics." This feminism, ironically but also dangerously, aspired to be strenuous, rigorous, and impersonal. It employed the martial arts of a combative vocabulary, the "manic generation of difficult terminology." Having entered the American academy, she felt, the fashionable new modes threatened to privilege theory over experience. She wrote: "We are moving towards a two-tiered system of 'higher' and 'lower' criticism, the higher concerned with the 'scientific' problems of form and structure, the 'lower' concerned with the 'humanistic' problems of content and interpretation." These distinctions, she feared, were assuming a gender fault line of a humanistic hermeneutics and a 'scientific' "hismeneutics."[41] Thus did Showalter turn the tables on the French feminists!

Showalter feared not only that language theory would confine feminism to an academic ghetto, but worried also that it would induce a linguistic eradication of the female subject. Under the assault of the deterministic habits of scientific criticism (and she included Marxism in this category), "the experience of women can easily disappear, become mute, invalid and invisible." Feminists, Showalter said, must not abandon their highest calling, to search the historical and literary record and reclaim the repressed voices of their sisters. "As women scholars in the 1970s," she wrote, "we have been given a great opportunity, a great intellectual challenge. The anatomy, the record, the poetics, the history, await our writing."[42]

While feminist literary theorists wondered about the audibility of woman's voice in their textual habitats, American historians were assuring women's greater visibility in the human past. As if taking up the Saussurean interest in what gets left out in language, women historians had little difficulty in defining what was missing in traditional historical narrative.[43] The proliferation of studies in women's history dominates the new directions in that subject in the 1970s. In all eras, regions, and classes the centrality of women in the decade's historical studies was unmistakable. It would be debated at length whether the record told a story of oppression and near obliteration of females in the mainstream of human experience or whether the new searches unearthed the evidence of heretofore unrecognized successes. Whatever the conclusions, historical scholarship gained significantly by the efforts. It gained in depth and breadth, in complexity and variety; and it gained in interest. Women's history brought new intellectual excitements to the field. As Sheila Ryan Johansson wrote in 1973: "Clio, the muse of history, is now a liberated woman."[44]

Amid the accumulating historical studies of women, some feminist historians felt the need for a greater theoretical precision in their work. They wanted history to step out of its empirical mode and reach conclusions about the nature of women's historical experience as seen especially in gender relations. Theory would also lead into questions of methodology. Were previous questions asked of the past appropriate or useful for women's history? Were different standards of measure now needed by which to assess progress and change in history? Was a new periodization called for? The theoretical questions would yield some provocative speculations, but they would also unearth dilemmas and contradictions. Theory gained most when it took on postmodernist problematics.

As in all academic fields, in history much feminist concern focused on undoing male influence in the profession. The problem entailed much more than neglect of women as important historical subjects. The problem was rooted in the conceptualization of history itself. Feminists rejected the notion of an objective and value-free history, for that notion simply disguised the reality of a universalistic male world view. Second, women's history reflected the pattern of an "assertive particularism" that Peter Novick found a dominant trend in 1960s and 1970s historiography. Thus it became axiomatic among many feminists that only feminists could write women's history. At times feminist theory could come very close to a mystification of women's special consciousness, invoked to overwrite the male inscriptions that had colored historical narrative previously. Such positioning though stood athwart other feminists' efforts to purge such proximate essentialism from all discourse on gender.[45]

Some feminists charged that categorization and periodization in history had always been normative male constructs. That is, men have defined history in terms of visible change denoted, for example, by political struggle and economic progress. History then found its major landmarks in technological change, wars, revolutions, and periodic shifts in power as denoted by presidential administrations. In contrast, women's lives seed to take on a kind of timelessness, the eternal cycle of the home and family. Woman thus became a trans-historical being removed from the dynamics and chronological markings of history. Those who defined this problem noted another incongruity— that women acquired a history only when they stepped out of their prescribed sphere and entered the world of men. But a useful women's history could hardly emerge from activity in which women are considered to be acting in a masculine way.[46]

Other feminist historians believed that historical analysis suffered from a gender culture and language that male historians had employed invidiously. As a case in point, feminist historians faulted works by Robert Riegel (his 1963 book *American Feminists*) and William O'Neill (his 1969 book *Everyone Was Brave: The Rise and Fall of Feminism in America*). These studies of reformers suffered, feminist critics believed, because the male authors honored in the feminists the characteristics of practicality, rationality, and intellectual analysis that had a male cultural resonance. They disparaged other characteristics of emotionalism, sentimentality, and irrationalism that suggested an endemic female nature.[47] But this kind of judgment landed feminists in a dilemma. They censured men who judged women by male norms, but to spare women that judgment, it would appear, they would have to sanction a legitimate alternative standard appropriate to the female gender. The women's movement in its early years, however, had often made it a defining ideological point to reject any gender dualism, any notion that women and men had innate differentiating characteristics.

Another contradiction confronted women historians. On the one hand, their subject, they said, demonstrated that women had long been the oppressed sex, victims of the enduring and hegemonic patriarchy in Western civilization. On the other hand, these historians wrote in celebration of the unrecognized women who had made important contributions to their times but had suffered unwarranted neglect by reason of male prejudice. Perhaps there was not necessarily a contradiction in these perspectives, but some feminists noted it and made it an opportunity to define women's history in light of it. Gerda Lerner thus observed that too much focus on victimization of women produced a picture of passivity and weakness in the face of patriarchy. "Such inquiry," she wrote "fails to elicit the positive and essential way in which women have functioned in history." And their ongoing contribution, she said, cannot be learned by emphasizing only their oppression. Lerner insisted that victimization is a term that derives from a male standard of measure. But the true history of women, Lerner argued, "is the history of their ongoing function in that male-defined world *on their own terms.*"[48] This perspective might place women's history on a better footing, but it had troubling implications. A women's movement that looked for female breakthroughs into professions like law, business, medicine, and higher education wanted precisely to have traditional male standards apply to them on an equal basis. They no longer wanted to measure their own success by the traditional "women's spheres."

Many feminist historians insisted that women constituted a distinct and special historical category, marked above all by their habitual state of oppression. They thus must be studied as such.[49] But among women historians and among some particularly looking for theoretical positions, a disinclination to employ holistic categories and terminology advanced in the 1970s. Lerner, for example, argued that comparing American women to slaves in the early nineteenth century greatly simplified a complex historical situation. Such rhetorical devices did not explain the paradoxical position of women. Situated throughout society, women had no power but were close to those who did—as wives of cabinet members, daughters of congressmen, sisters of businessmen. They were exploited workers but exploiters themselves. As upholders of custom, law, and religion, they played a conservative role, but they also joined and activated many reformist and even revolutionary organizations.[50]

Feminist theory in history became most persuasive when it acknowledged paradox and complexity. It gained, in fact, when it assumed a poststructuralist skepticism towards such terms as "oppression" when applied as an inclusive explanation for women's history over extended periods of time. The term certainly had meaning, but it had greater precision when deconstructed into its pluralistic embodiments. Ann Gordon and her colleagues made the point that "oppression" served sometimes not to create the bonds of womanhood but to establish women's separation from each other. The slave woman and the plantation mistress both experienced oppression, but their race differentiated that oppression and kept barriers between them. Gordon wrote: "Focusing entirely on the bond women share by virtue of sex, the concept of oppression does little to explain the dynamics of either woman's life or the historical conditions underlying it. It does violence to the lives of black women and men under slavery and sidesteps white women's role in that enslavement."[51] In a manner suggestive of a Foucauldian analysis of power and control, Gordon rejected the idea of women as a special caste, oppressed and thus removed from the larger dynamics of history and social change. Instead, she said, one must "look at the interactions between their 'sphere' and the larger society," in the multiple, diverse, and complex points of contact in which they both perpetuated and subverted the controlling structure.[52] Women's true historical experience was not accessible by any logocentric containment.

The theoretical discussions were not without specific issue. Throughout the 1970s women historians in America engaged each other in opposing interpretations of their subject. The most suggestive encounter focused on women in the nineteenth century. Historians of women had begun to discover a "women's culture." It derived from the close and often intimate experiences of women with each other, experiences that specified a special space within the larger matrices of the society and created a defining moment for American womanhood. Female comradeship, formed across interfamily ties, club organizations, and other places of personal contact, came to have a new fascination for historians of women. But describing the larger significance of women's culture proved to be a political battle of its own.

For those who patterned American gender in terms of a stark male oppression of women, the new focus on women's culture brought mostly discomfort. Positing a male hegemony in the nineteenth century, these critics saw women's culture indicative of the displacement of American women from the dominant power arrangements in American society and their isolation from its determining dynamics. Ellen Dubois thus referred to a "public" sphere of American life controlled by men and a "private" sphere into which fell the various coteries of female activity. She furthermore found the sequestered women's culture lacking in any effective oppositional content and thus posing no challenge to the existing order.[53]

To DuBois, the women's suffrage movement then took on special significance. It moved outside the confinements of family, which she saw as the essence of male oppression of females, and sought to break into the public sphere, challenging the essential configurations of the gender polarity. "By demanding a permanent, public role for all women," DuBois wrote, "suffragists began to demolish the absolute, sexually defined barrier marking the public world of men off from the private world of women."[54] Now women began to define ways to relate to society independent of their family ties. Furthermore, DuBois believed, other major, potential breakthroughs attended the suffrage movement—a new self-consciousness for women and a new sense of identity. Hence, while women's culture signified an accepting and even conservative posture of women in the nineteenth century, women's politics, i.e. the suffrage movement, offered the hope of a "revolutionary possibility." To DuBois, genuine feminism stood at odds with women's culture and she wished to highlight the political as primary in the history of feminism.[55]

To other women historians, DuBois's focus on the political seemed too constricting.[56] These viewpoints usually stressed the need to move beyond the male/female dichotomy, which left mostly a portrayal of women as victims, and to locate the various expressions of an autonomous women's culture, rich and potent, and the very basis of any possibility of a feminist movement in the United States. Carroll Smith-Rosenberg pressed this view very hard. She welcomed the new insights and the new resources supplied by social history in the 1960s and believed they confirmed the importance of the "nonpolitical"—schools, places of work, churches and religious activities, hospitals, prisons, brothels—as the arenas for fresh insights on women's history. For one thing, they helped break the male periodization that prevailed in political history and that defined women by a hierarchy of significance appropriate mostly to the male public sphere. The shift to the extrapolitical, to women's culture, Smith-Rosenberg described as the "New Women's History" and she associated it with the French *Annales* School, black history, and other efforts to give voice to the previously silent forces in history.[57]

Smith-Rosenberg and other women believed that women's culture provided a new appreciation of women in the nineteenth century, but they insisted as well that women's culture made an emphatically progressive and reformist contribution. Female solidarity belonged in any definition of feminism, they believed; it even served as the necessary basis for any women's movement. The major feminist groups and the major feminist leaders, they believed, all found a prior experience in women's solidarity that prepared them for their political work. "The greatest strength they gained from this experience, I would suggest," said Smith-Rosenberg, "was to define themselves first as women and second as reformers." [58]

A complex picture was emerging in women's history at the end of the 1970s, one that reflected postmodernist discomfort with totalizing paradigms and their stark dialectical oppositions and hegemonic colorations. The 1970s' presentation of women showed a Foucault-like social construction in which a multiplicity of contending forces interact and in which the controlling force confronts countervailing spheres and subversions in concurrent interactions. Thus, for example, when *Feminist Studies* at the end of the decade surveyed the question of women's politics versus women's culture in women's history, Mari Jo Buhle illustrated how these new perspectives forced reconsideration of traditional subjects in women's history. The modern feminist, she pointed out, might find distasteful or disturbing the sentiments of motherhood, the home, and moral purity—of domesticity, in short—that flourished among the female reformers of the late nineteenth century (as for example in the Women's Christian Temperance Union). These principles, she noted, have even appeared as "villains" in the history of feminism. But it was just this tenacious culture in which women flourished that propelled them into the political arena of the suffrage struggle. This culture effected a new feminist consciousness, one that conducted its own subversions.[59] So likewise did the various feminist strategies in American scholarship. They, too, in postmodernist fashion, undermined normative and holistic structures based on universalist, male determinations.

seven

Debating Black

At the end of the 1960s, the black movement in the United States stood at a crossroads. The civil rights struggles of the 1950s and early 1960s had addressed America's most glaring shortcomings. It had effected a "Second Reconstruction" by moving through the courts and national legislatures in the effort to secure equal rights for all citizens. Passage of the 1964 Voting Rights Act and the 1965 Civil Rights Act signalled most dramatically the effort to secure equality before the law and a larger entry into public life for African-Americans. But already the movement had taken on a different emphasis. Themes of Black Nationalism and Black Power looked beyond law and called on black people to stress their autonomy, their own cultural identity, and their historical roots in Africa. Powerful voices, such as that of Malcolm X, spoke to the urban poor of America and to an awakened younger generation, to whom changes in the law addressed only part of their concerns. The explosion of the inner cities, beginning with the Watts district of Los Angeles in 1965, painfully and frighteningly reminded Americans of the desperate and frustrated conditions of the ghetto inhabitants. The violent deaths of Malcolm and Martin Luther King, Jr., also created a need for new leadership and challenged the program for the 1970s.

By this time certainly black culture had become a major focus. Many liberals believed that the civil rights movement had fulfilled its political mission and now must consolidate its gains. Many other sympathetic whites feared the new militant expressions of the late 1960s and, save for some tenacious romantic leftists, did not identify with such groups as the Black Panthers and their insurrectionary rhetoric and activity. But culture was a field awaiting appropriation. Sometimes it carried clear and heavy political purposes. Said Ron Karenga: "There must be a cultural revolution before there is the violent revolution."[1] To many, the movement known as the Black Aesthetic answered such high hopes and expectations.

The Black Aesthetic built on important cultural efforts of the 1960s. It included the Black Arts program, previously discussed, that forged a union of artists and masses in major cities and promoted the idea of a self-consciously distinct and meaningful black culture in the United States. The poems and plays of LeRoi Jones (later Imamu Amiri Baraka) best defined the power and separatist motif of the new expressions. New journals also supported the effort: *Negro Digest* (renamed *Black World* in 1970), *The Journal of Black Poetry, The Black Scholar, Black Theater, Black Books Bulletin.* Distinctiveness also inspired the efforts by students at American colleges and universities to establish black studies programs, a movement that gained consent rapidly in the first half of the 1970s. The founding of the National Council for Black Studies in 1976 registered those gains. As early as 1971 Yale historian John Blassingame could issue an edited book called *New Perspectives in Black Studies.*

The black culture movement addressed the question of identity and image for black people in America. It answered a universal complaint by black social and cultural critics that American public culture had reconstructed black life in terms of the stereotypes that most serviced its own racist ends. The movement also responded to a situation wherein the television and film media made African-Americans virtually nonexistent or at best the carefully fashioned types that blended with white middle-class norms. Thus, along with black cultural organizations, there emerged the National Black Media Coalition and the Black Citizens for Fair Media. Both kinds of organizations reflected a rising sense of racial consciousness and a clear resolve that blacks rediscover and define their own uniting identity.[2]

The publication of a major anthology, *The Black Aesthetic,* under the editorial direction of Addison Gayle, Jr., signified the ascendancy of cultural nationalism in the black movement. Contributors (the selections included earlier voices of the Harlem Renaissance) addressed the categories of "Theory," "Music," "Poetry," "Drama," and "Fiction" and made this 1971 manifesto a cultural landmark of the early decade.

The Black Aesthetic clearly bore the markings of 1960s passion and militancy. Its program was no formalist project. Black literature and art were not invoked for merely aesthetic ends and in some instances were specifically conscripted to the service of a higher political calling. Karenga, an influential voice in black nationalism and founder in the middle 1960s of the militant organization US, merged art and politics in common cause. He asserted that only social and political criteria could judge the usefulness of any art; artistic considerations alone did not suffice. Quite simply, he wrote, "all art must reflect and support the Black Revolution," and any that does not assist in this end is invalid, no matter how nicely contrived are its artistic forms. Furthermore, he insisted, revolutionary art must be collective in spirit and message. Karenga rejected any notions of a special genius in the creative process and any notion of "art for art's sake." Black art, Karenga demanded, "must be from the people and must be returned to the people." It must demonstrate commitment to revolution and must justify its usefulness to the extent that it inspires such commitment in its audience.[3]

Those sentiments found support among major black American writers, John Oliver Killens for one. He wrote the novels *And Then We Heard the Thunder* (1963), *'Sippi* (1967), and *Cotillion* (1971). He, too, endorsed a socialist realist position for black art. "It is time for some black writers, the more the merrier, to move from social protest to affirmation and revolution. Every black writer worth his bread is a revolutionary of sorts." Killens said that he always wanted his fiction "to rock the boat, to change the world." Black America, he added, needed new myths and legends; it has been asked too long to identify with white heroes. Killens invoked the names of Nat Turner, Frederick Douglass, Denmark Vesey, and Harriet Tubman.[4]

A stark black/white dualism recurs in *The Black Aesthetic*. The Kerner Commission report of 1968 had described a United States virtually divided into separate black and white societies. Its conclusions came as no surprise to black leaders, political and cultural alike. For these divisions obtained in the world of art, too. The formulators of *The Black Aesthetic*, then, took as given what Hoyt Fuller, editor of *Black World*, described as "the irreconcilable conflict between the black writer and the white critic." Black writers and critics, he said, believed that black culture had not received recognition in the white literary establishment. But that fact merely reflected the larger truth that "the two races are residents of two separate and naturally antagonistic worlds," all the well-meaning rhetoric of "one country" and "one people" notwithstanding. If black art attains authenticity, Fuller said, then it will reflect the colonial status of blacks within their own country. It will lose that authenticity to the extent that black artists seek recognition and approval by whites. Black art must reflect its "very special ethos." Citing the growing recognition of this need, Fuller referred to the Organization of Black American Culture and its work in Chicago, particularly the writers' workshops sponsored by this group, and their efforts to invest their work with the "distinctive styles and rhythms and colors of the ghetto."[5]

From Watts to Harlem, art projects of this kind flourished. Painters used neo-primitive and expressionist styles to invoke the bold patterning and bright colors familiar in African textiles. As Barbara Rose observed in 1970: "Such artists wish to establish an autonomous black art movement closely linked with black separatist politics. . . . Directing their art exclusively to the needs of a black public, they reject the modern European tradition as a decadent style serving a white bourgeois Establishment." Much of this work, she observed, recalled the socialist realism of the 1930s. "Their themes stress values basic to the black social struggle: they paint families united or idealized workers and leaders of the black community like Malcolm X and Martin Luther King."[6]

A separate black art would seem to imply a separate black standard of criticism. Darwin Turner, an important black scholar, described, and gave qualified endorsement to a new group of black critics that had just that end in mind. They demanded that literature be judged according to aesthetic standards peculiar to African-American culture. *Negro Digest* in October 1969 had created a symposium on black culture that allowed contributors to explore these possibilities. Turner seemed to validate the separatist motif of the Black Aesthetic when he commented that deference to white critical standards had prevented black artists from realizing full self-definition. He wanted black art now to move from imitation to innovation.[7] Often black commentators mistrusted the claims, by whites, that all art should be judged by impersonal, "universalist" standards. Such pretense, they believed, invariably removed black work from serious consideration.[8]

These concerns all reinforced a preoccupation with exceptionalism among those who favored black nationalism. That emphasis extended into academia, too, not only in black studies programs, but within academic disciplines as well. There, too, an "assertive particularism" took hold, as in the history profession, for example. A separatist consciousness enshrouded black history with a kind of mystique, such that only a black scholar, putatively, could effectively study that subject. The new separatist consciousness precluded whites, but also cast suspicion on some black historians themselves. Black history, it seemed, should reflect a certain ideological position. Older black historians who emphasized the progress of the race, for example, might be faulted for "Americanizing" their subject and internalizing a dominant progressive white outlook. In the era of ghetto unrest these accounts were judged to be irrelevant.[9]

Nonetheless, much black history of the 1970s did have a certain celebrating quality about it. It treated blacks as strong subjects, tenaciously holding to their own and preserving a rich and memorable way of life in the face of all that threatened to erode it. Thus these studies stressed the positive and minimized anything that suggested pathology. Particularly important to this recovery were the vitality and will-to-life conveyed in mass black culture. Religion, music, and slave folklore conveyed a communal consciousness that preserved a special racial culture. The black family, too, emerged as key institution in the race's survival. Indeed, themes of resistance and autonomy in black history informed the perspectives of 1970s historians on their subject. But these historical hymns of praise, Peter Novick observed, slighted aspects of black history and culture that had troubled earlier black intellectuals.[10]

All the intellectual and academic subjects that honored a specific black experience found a striking parallel among the American black populace. To many who responded positively to the expressions of black pride, Africa itself had a particular resonance and symbolized a particular centrality for blacks with differentiated histories in the United States. From the mid-1960s on, the wearing of dashikis, bubas, and caftans caught on, suggesting to others a certain militant nationalism. The "Afro" or "natural" hair style became widely prevalent, however dubiously it represented authentic African tradition. The mystique of the black soul gained tangible references in "soul food" and "soul music," and attained such an omnipresence that these items were easily commercialized. Africa Ltd., a crafts shop in New York, sold African objects of all kinds—musical instruments from Ethiopia and Nigeria, masks from the Ivory Coast, games, dolls, and carved wood chest sets. In a report from 1970, the proprietor said that he could not keep these items in stock, so much did his customers demand them.[11]

Language also gained a new primacy in black cultural nationalism. Malcolm X had urged the study of Swahili. Though an African East Coast language and thus not indigenous to the West Coast origin of most African-Americans, it was judged to be an African lingua franca that boasted a significant literary tradition in prose and poetry.[12] "Black English," too, now aspired to public acceptance and academic recognition. Its defenders sometimes used the Black Aesthetic for legitimation of the special speech patterns, grammar, and syntax of Black English for they too helped define the unique and special in black culture. Language, supporters said, helps define an individual's consciousness and transmits reality in a particular way to its users.[13] J. L. Dillard in his noted study *Black English* made a special effort to demonstrate the African basis of this dialect, against considerable scholarship that made it derivative of various white groups.[14]

It might appear at first glance that black culture could furnish a rallying cry for all committed to the black cause. It suggested a common unity, a tradition waiting to be recovered and displayed with pride, an identity that transcended class and region. But black culture supplied no such common base. In fact, it produced an extensive discussion in the early to middle 1970s and after plentiful diagnosis from many sides the notion fell into a deconstructed state that rendered problematic the efforts to conceptualize black America on any holistic terms.

The case of Ron Karenga supplies an instructive and baffling illustration. Karenga had made himself a student of African languages and promoted the study of Swahili among his followers and among residents in Watts. He had earned an M.A. at UCLA. He wore African-style dress. Members of his group US practiced a self-made African religion and adopted African names for their own identities (Karenga using "Maulana").[15] In the middle 1970s, though, Karenga, who had said that the·cultural revolution must precede the violent one, turned his critical attention to the black culture movement. At that time, Karenga found himself in prison, following a conviction for felonious assault while supporters were raising money for his legal defense.

Karenga's essays in *Black Scholar* showed that he had not abandoned at all his commitment to revolution. Now, however, he believed that cultural nationalism weakened that commitment in the black community. The celebration of culture, Karenga warned, threatened to reduce the movement to a comfortable retreat into rhetoric and symbol. Traditional dress and hair styles have an assuring appeal, he asserted, but they could offer only ineffective surrogates for the revolution born of class and racial oppression. "Cultural atavism," as Karenga dismissed the fixation on tradition, could dangerously divert or sabotage the movement by its distinctly "unrevolutionary" character. "We must attack and eliminate mysticism and spookism and reject the use of soul as a substitute for concrete and substantive achievement," he wrote.[16]

Karenga himself had clearly committed to a Marxist foundation of the black movement. To that extent he placed great stress on theory and ideology, the essences of any movement that knew its course and could follow it through. Ideology alone could be useful in opposition to the dominant society. Karenga therefore de-emphasized "perception," which he associated with "soul" and its associated mystique of the ghetto. Instead he validated "conception," which he associated with an intellectual apprehension of the social totality. To the cultural enthusiasts he put the matter directly: "We can pretend street life is the ultimate in awareness and achievement or we can reject that life, its lowliness, lies, and self-illusions and begin to challenge and change the conditions of our existence through active and informed struggle."[17]

Black nationalism, Karenga insisted, could supply only a partial understanding of revolutionary needs. Revealing a debt to Georg Lukács and Western Marxism, Karenga wanted to link black revolution to appropriate ideas of totality. The cultural recovery, he believed, could yield only a species of self-understanding that correlated to bourgeois foregrounding of the self in all modes of thinking. One could return to the primacy of class, and the focus on capitalism as the singular object of revolutionary focus, Karenga believed, only by seizing the social totality. He wrote: "Self-knowledge becomes no more than self-deception if it does not include a thorough knowledge of the society that shaped us, affects us and transforms our basic social and historical identity." Ultimately then, Karenga urged, the only meaningful reality is the USA, "the *heart* and *gut* of the capitalist world." The plight of black America finds meaning only in the context of that complex whole. Liberation can proceed only through that entity and not through the side eddies of African tradition.[18]

Karenga had some surprising allies in his case against cultural nationalism as the foundation of the black movement. The Black Muslims, for one, wanted no part of it. Perceiving the black subculture as the wreckage of white society, the Nation of Islam offered no endorsement of black life as found. Calling on their own expression of a puritan ethic, the Muslims posed against the ghetto—its culture of poverty, its hedonism, violence, and degradation—a code of rigorous self-discipline, of work and morality. The Nation's leader, Elijah Muhammad, disdained soul food and dismissed popular ghetto fare as the "Great Poison Dishes." The cultural renaissance had no more appeal to Muhammad. Black Studies won no endorsement and the cult of Africa elicited only rebuke. Muhammad wished to exorcise from the black American mind its fascination with African clothing and effects—"superficial fake images of Blackness."[19]

Both the Black Muslims and the Black Panthers believed that the black culture boom flourished at the behest and the interest of whites. A Black Panther spokesman spurned the cultural renaissance as "a bourgeois-capitalist scheme" to divert the assault on political institutions. The Panthers now embraced a Marxist-Leninist ideology and suspected all devices of the capitalists to divert the revolution. White involvement in the cultural revival exploited the commercial market for soul food and soul music, they claimed. Furthermore, African culture, they believed, carried no revolutionary messages into the ghetto. Hence, too, it appealed predominantly to the black middle class. Eldridge Cleaver and other Black Panthers saw mostly university-educated blacks as the instigators of cultural nationalism and, as one said, "we don't mean to get hung up studying Swahili for the next sixteen semesters while we are being oppressed, suffer unemployment, low paying jobs . . . and police brutality."[20]

The cultural-Marxist nexus that stood out among black revolutionists reflected some of the militancy of the late 1960s and its rhetorical overkill. But black memory did make some partisans skeptical of alliance with the Left. They pointed out that blacks, and black artists as well, had always faced racist deprivation in the Communist and Socialist parties and their various front groups. For these white-controlled organizations black identity had no significance and a preoccupation with class and economics ignored racism as the root cause of black oppression. Those who issued these warnings could cite the experiences of major black writers like Richard Wright and Langston Hughes who, often in painful memory, had broken from the radical Left.[21]

The leadership of the National Association for the Advancement of Colored People, America's venerable black organization, also stood aloof from the black culture movement. Its long-standing opposition to racial segregation in the United States, which had led it through important court victories, placed the organization at odds with the separatist themes of the nationalists. The NAACP did not warm to Black Studies programs in the universities and betrayed no sentimentality about Black English. Its spokesmen, in fact, perceived in almost every effort to define a special black genre in the arts a naive celebration of ghetto life. Hollywood's new string of black movies in the seventies provided a case in point. At best, NAACP spokesmen said, the mystification of "soul" and the appropriation of African symbols provided an escapist fantasy and a dubious basis for genuine black pride.[22] But the losses outweighed the gains. The case against cultural nationalism came in two essays in the NAACP's journal, *The Crisis*.

Ralph Ellison provided one of the replies. Ellison, author of *The Invisible Man* (1952), widely judged to be one of the great American novels of the twentieth century, provided what could be described as the black humanist critique of black nationalism. By no means did Ellison divorce black art from the social struggle that engaged all African-Americans. Hence, his criticism could not be described as proffering a strictly formalist aesthetic. But Ellison wanted very much to define how art could contribute to the social question and he warned that it could not contribute effectively if it made the social question dominant to its purposes.

Ellison feared that a preoccupation with revolutionary "black art" led black artists to lapse into a heavy socialist realism in which content—image, subject, the offending reality—replace technique and artistic mastery. Ellison insisted that the artist's mission is to bring a new visual order into the world. He must challenge an audience to see the world differently. But that mission, he believed, should give a first priority to aesthetic consciousness, which must in turn affect the social. Ellison summarized, in sympathetic manner, the dilemma faced by the black artist:

> How then, he asks himself, does even an artist steeped in the most advanced lore of his craft and most passionately concerned with solving the more advanced problems of painting as *painting* address himself to the perplexing question of bringing his art to bear upon the task (never so urgent as now) of defining Negro American identity, of presenting its claims for recognition and for justice? He feels, in brief, a near-unresolvable conflict between his urge to leave his mark upon the world through art and his ties to his group and its claims upon him.[23]

Ellison, on the subject of art, spoke for the same integrationist standards that the NAACP defended in American society. He feared that black art suffered by accepting the myth of a separate black culture, one that led to aesthetic isolationism, a rejection of any "white" standards of creativity. Ellison's work served as a reminder that American culture includes black culture, that America has no meaning without the black person's place in it. The dualism in separatist ideology, he warned, gives legitimacy, on the one hand, to the notion of "a pure mainstream culture 'unpolluted' by any trace of Negro American style or idiom." And on the other hand, it leads black artists to forsake the aesthetic tradition of the West and to present their art only in terms of stark sociological content.[24]

Ellison made his essay a celebration of Romare Bearden. He saw in Bearden's paintings a triumph of technique, one that transformed his Harlem subjects in so striking a way as to force his audience to make new discoveries about them. Bearden, said Ellison, had decided that in order to possess his world "artistically" he had to confront it not through propaganda or sentimentality, "but through the finest techniques and traditions of painting." Ellison seemed to direct his remarks to the voices of black nationalism. Bearden, he urged "sought to recreate his Harlem in the light of his painter's vision, and thus he avoided the defeats suffered by many of the aspiring painters of that period who seemed to have felt that they had only to produce out of a mood of protest and despair the scenes and surfaces of Harlem, in order to win artistic mastery and accomplish social transfiguration." Ellison discerned in Bearden's painting artistic techniques that recalled Western artists like Giotto, Pieter de Hooch, Picasso, and Mondrian. Bearden, wrote Ellison, used the eye of the painter, not that of the sociologist, and he demonstrated the irrelevance of race as a restricting factor in art.[25]

Veteran civil rights leader Bayard Rustin took an even more oppositional stance to black cultural nationalism. "There is no such thing as a black artist," he wrote. He dismissed as vulgarity the effort to make art the subordinate vehicle of any social or political cause. Rustin lamented that young movement artists settled for an inferior art product by joining their enthusiasm to related political causes. But, he said, no art exists "independent of artistic standards." Thus, he explained, it would be easy to describe the powerful Negro spirituals as a cultural response to oppression. To be sure, said Rustin, they had their political purposes, but he insisted that "the spiritual came first of all out of their [the slaves'] own religious experience, and the convergence with politics was secondary."[26]

Rustin used the occasion of his *Crisis* article to issue several caveats regarding the aggressive exceptionalism that had taken over discussions about black culture. He believed that Black Studies academic programs yielded to ideology at the expense of truth. He scotched the notion that only black painters or writers could realistically portray the black experience. What, then, should we say of Alan Paton's *Cry, the Beloved Country,* "a work which sensitized us all to the horror of South Africa"? After a long career on the front line of agitation for the black cause, which included an early membership in the Young Communist League, Rustin's commitment to the intrinsic humanism of art assumed a special forcefulness. "The painter, the writer, the singer, and the dancer," he urged, "ultimately reflect the way in which our people live. And to the degree that they are good artists, they do not lie. To the degree that they set up an ideology, an apologia for the black experience and distort that black experience into their own preconceived notions, to that degree do they destroy us all."[27]

The quest for an essentialist Black Aesthetic confronted another obstacle when it was queried by the new literary theory. In the middle and late 1970s literary scholar Houston Baker wrote some essays on black American literature and then collected them into his book *The Journey Back*. Baker said that he appreciated the literary goals of the Black Aesthetic movement, but he perceived also its limitations. Its spokesmen, he acknowledged, recognized the power of the word, but seemed to believe that they could will a black nation into being by verbal fiat, by exhortation. "The goal they propose," he wrote, "is rebirth. But the rebirth represented is an extremely lexical one: the words strive to recreate a primordial black logos, or word, through sheer lyricism and assertiveness. God, the artist, and the 'holy, holy, black man' are possible agents of a new creation."[28]

Baker feared that the Black Aesthetic movement served to credit prejudicial attitudes toward black writing, charges that it reflected more of expres-

127

sion, more of "sound and fury," than of substance. But he worried also that the emphasis on a unique and holistic black culture might obscure a richer and more complicated tradition of black writing, one that did indeed mark the uniqueness of the black experience in the United States. It became a critical question, then, how that tradition, that style, that underlying meaning, might be uncovered. The key for Baker lay in appropriating for black literature a particular linguistic methodology. As he remarked in his introduction, "the research in which I am engaged . . . has as its end a method of analysis that will explain *how* black narrative texts written in English preserve and communicate culturally unique meanings. I am seeking a way—beyond verbal fiat— to substantiate a particular point of view on black American culture and art."[29] His efforts made *The Journey Back* itself a significant intellectual document in black writing.

Baker found a key to black literary meaning in structuralism,[30] but, as we shall see, his interpretive strategies moved him into a deconstructive mode of analysis. Culture, said Baker, is analogous to linguistic discourse. Language consists of an organizing unity higher or "beyond" the individual words and sentences by which it operates. These constructs constitute language's special rules, principles, and conventional procedures. They determine the function of language in a particular society. Baker employed some technical Saussurean language, but he clarified his intentions by the analogy of a chess game. The board, the plays, and the several moves, he said, comprise a "game" of chess only when set against the background of known "rules" by which the game is played. The various moves have no meaning apart from those rules, and to the uninitiated observer they make no sense. Baker also borrowed from Clifford Geertz to establish his strategy of "thick description" for undertaking the journey back into black literature.[31]

Baker addressed the problem of the self as a matter of special significance for black history. Borrowing from French psychoanalytic theorist Jacques Lacan, he described the attainment of selfhood as a prerequisite of language. Baker accepted the notion that language constitutes the self, a notion he wanted to observe within the culture of slavery. Baker thus could write of the slave that, in pursuit of identity, "he had first to seize the word. His being had to erupt from nothingness. Only by grasping the word could he engage in the speech acts that would ultimately define his selfhood." But the language he must appropriate was the language of the host culture, that of the white Americans. The African-American must then establish and preserve a differentiated self through the peculiar encodings he could inscribe on the words within that language. Black narrative, Baker described, thus took on double meanings, overlaps, and modified conceptual fields. Black language, like the operations of a Foucauldian power structure, hosted subverting elements that dismantled the linguistic hegemony of the dominant group. For black narrative, subtext would always disclose a more functional meaning than text.[32]

The Journey Back briefly reviews black American literature, beginning with glimpses of Phillis Wheatley and Gustavus Vassa. But Baker's discussion of the prominent nineteenth-century African-American, the ex-slave Frederick Douglass, shows the many problems of black cultural history that Baker confronted in his linguistic turn. For Douglass's life, as revealed especially in his own famous autobiography, is a struggle constituted in language, Baker argued. Thus, Douglass's owner, Mr. Auld, seeks domination over him by defining him as "nigger." Baker raised this matter to universal significance. "Mr. Auld is a representation of those writers who felt that by superimposing the cultural sign *nigger* on vibrant human beings like Douglass, they would be able to control the meaning and possibilities of life in America."[33] Auld, of course, also seeks to deny Douglass the possibilities of any linguistic subversions by preventing his learning to read.

But Douglass' story takes a special twist. His mistress, Mrs. Auld, in allegiance to her Christian evangelical imperatives, sees to his learning the English language. That undertaking empowers Douglass' construction of self (Baker: "the slave can arrive at a sense of being only through language"). But it is also true that this passage to self-realization occurs through the white media of the dominant culture. Douglass then appropriates those norms; he employs the language of the controlling system to establish his own freedom and to take up the cause of liberation for his own race. Douglass, in short, must seize on a split in the dominant language system—one that pronounces "nigger" and one that upholds Christian humanism.[34]

But at what cost? Baker asks. What has become of the authentic slave voice and its representations? For once literacy has been achieved, the black self, even as sounded in Douglass's *Narrative*, begins to distance itself from the slave quarters and their oral-aural culture. Baker observes: "The voice of the unwritten self, once it is subjected to the linguistic codes, literary conventions, and audience expectations of a literate population, is perhaps never again the authentic voice of black American slavery."[35] In the rest of his study Baker looked to black writers like Charles Chesnutt and Richard Wright in a further quest for the authentic black voice, pursuing the double meanings of the black narration that encode messages undetectable to the differently acculturated white reader.[36]

Baker for African-Americans helped define, as did Showalter, Gilbert, and Gubar for women, techniques of recovery and tactics of subversion. They gave a special feature in the 1970s to the larger tradition of dissent in America and they anticipated further efforts in the next decade.[37]

The Black Aesthetic represented a quest for essentialism, for the defining features and experience of a particular historical experience in America and the means of capturing it artistically. By the middle 1970s, the movement had spent its force and a political focus returned to primacy. However, any possibility of a holistic rendering of black culture proved hopelessly chimerical when another issue emerged into the full light of day at the end of the 1970s. The issue in question concerned sex and gender relations in black America. It fractured the community of black writers and intellectuals and it created wounds that angered, wounds that hurt.

The simmering subject came to a boil in 1978 when a twenty-six-year-old black woman published *Black Macho and the Myth of the Superwoman*. Michele Wallace's book began in resentment. It looked back to the "Movement" of the 1960s and recovered unpleasant memories—of middle-class white women in eager pursuit of the black men with whom they teamed in the civil rights efforts in the South. It also told of black men all too willing to take on sexual relations with them. Furthermore, Wallace charged, few black women had any significance at all in the struggle for their race. Now late in the day, Wallace wanted to ask the question, "where do we fit in?"[38]

What Wallace went on to write in *Black Macho* brought a response of bitter reaction from black men. Indeed, some cutting words gave her book its rhetorical edge. Black women, Wallace wrote, have long seen black men as "cripples," and they refused to take seriously the ways that, in recent years, their quest for masculinity had taken shape. These aspersions undercut Wallace's own efforts to trace sympathetically the impact of slavery on the black male in America, by which Wallace located the roots of the contemporary problem—the long history of racism in America. For in slavery, said Wallace, began the deprivation of black manhood. The male father could not present himself as an authority figure to his wife and children and slavery would stamp forever on him a resentment of his impotence, a resentment he took out against the one person that could do nothing about it, the black woman.[39]

After slavery, by Wallace's account, the black man made pursuit of the white female a governing motivation. He pursued her because the white man would not let him have her. And to raise the frightful specter of the racial/sexual connection, whites created the image of the Buck—the brutal, violent, and virile black male, the embodiment of primal lust. This history made the sixties understandable, Wallace believed. Now came the time when the black man could collect on his debts, hurt the white man in the most acute way. Making his way with white flesh, wrote Wallace, meant more to the black man than freedom or equality, which were merely the facade of the civil rights movement. So the black gained his masculinity, seized a trophy of war, and left the black woman with no resale value at all.[40]

Wallace wrote a definitively personal book. She described her own "middle-class" upbringing and "extremely protected" environment. But the seventies came, and with it the discovery of the ghetto. She could not resist the romanticism of it all and she threw herself into it, going where black was truly beautiful. Her disenchantment gives *Black Macho* much of its flavor. She would thereafter see the ghetto as a scene of powerlessness and degradation. And she would concur with other black critics who saw in the invention of the glamorous ghetto the ploys of the white culture. For that culture now conceded to the black man a certain form of masculinity—that of the tough drug runner, the flashy hustler, the slick dude. Witness the blaxploitation films of the seventies—*Shaft, Superfly*. The manhood that America finally conceded to black men was the manhood of a psychopath. This masculinity, Wallace wrote, "was flashy and attention-attracting like a zoot suit. Black men kicking white men's asses, fucking white women, and stringing black women along in a reappearance of the brutal Buck on the silver screen. Black men in big green hats, high-heeled shoes, and mink, with 'five white bitches' around the corner turning tricks for them."[41]

But to make this curious twist understandable, Wallace believed, one had to see the flip side of black macho, the black superwoman. She too came from the situation of slavery, as much the invention of the black man as of the white. To explain his powerlessness, the black man had to invent a woman who dominated him, who traded favors with the white man—the slave master who owned her, the employer who now hired her—and who went on to get more education and earn more money than he did. "We had driven him to alcohol, to drugs, to crime, to every bad thing he had ever done to harm himself or his family because our eyes had not reflected his manhood," wrote Wallace. The black superwoman was made to feel guilty for all of this.[42]

Few could react to *Black Macho* with anything like cool detachment. Some, with reluctance, conceded that Wallace had touched a raw nerve. One contributor to a forum on the subject of black male/female relations, presented by *The Black Scholar* journal, remarked that these relations had been corroding for a half-century and despaired at "this sorry state of affairs between the sexes."[43] Said another: "Terrible things, on a scale unprecedented in the past, are happening between black men and women. However flawed the works, we cannot argue away this message."[44] Nor could one easily ignore Wallace. An observer said of *Black Macho* that "it has attracted probably more attention in the consciousness-raising industry (i.e. T.V. and newspapers) than any other book on this topic."[45] The January 1979 issue of *Ms.* magazine presented a front-cover close-up of Michele Wallace and included lengthy extracts from her book. Thus the wide publicity redoubled the anger of those offended by *Black Macho*, for they believed it a damaging account. One critic called it "one of the most serious threats to black people since the slave trade."[46] Another labeled it "one of the most vicious, slanderous attacks against both black men and women, and indeed against the Black Liberation movement, on record."[47] Nor did the complaints issue only from black men. In a *New York Times Book Review* offering, English professor June Jordan, citing the book's "unprecedented promotion and publicity," called it "nothing more than a fractious, divisive tract," and added to charges made by others that it suffered from generalities and poor scholarship.[48]

A few things might be noted. First, Wallace did not singularly ignite the feud. Recurringly in the 1970s a black feminist voice was making itself heard, and it had some grievances it wanted to direct at black men. Some of the fuel for the new black feminist consciousness came from the depictions of brutal black men that stand out graphically in the novels of Alice Walker—e.g. *The Third Life of Grange Copeland* (1970), *Meridian* (1977), and later *The Color Purple* (1982).[49] On another front, Barbara Sizemore in a 1973 article systematically denounced the Nation of Islam for its patriarchal, exclusionist, and mercenary posture toward women. Nor did she disguise bitter feelings toward black leaders who married white women. She named James Farmer, Senator Edward Brooke, Harry Belafonte, James Forman, and Julius Lester among others. "What does this say to black women?" she asked.[50] And in her 1974 autobiography Marxist/revolutionist Angela Davis described how male leaders like Karenga accused her of doing "a man's job" and how he and his like specified that women should not be leaders. Here began for Davis what she said would become "a constant problem in my political life." She elaborated, with no little sense of annoyance:

> I became acquainted very early with the widespread presence of an unfortunate syndrome among some Black male activists—namely to confuse their political activity with an assertion of their maleness. They saw—and some continue to see—-Black manhood as something separate from Black womanhood. These men view Black women as a threat to their attainment of manhood—especially those Black women who take initiative and work to become leaders in their own right. The constant harangue by the US [Karenga's organization] men was that I needed to redirect my energies and use them to give my man strength and inspiration so that he might more effectively contribute his talents to the struggle for Black liberation.[51]

Second, throughout the decade black intellectuals had been addressing statistics that showed black women significantly outnumbering black men in the United States population. The statistics also told of rising numbers of single-parent, female-led families. At the same time figures also pointed to greater numbers of black women than men holding professional and technical jobs. These trends were very frequently addressed with the controversial 1965 "Moynihan Report" in mind. That year Assistant Secretary of Labor Daniel Moynihan wrote for the Johnson administration "The Negro Family: The Case for National Action." The report pointed to the "tangle of pathology" in the northern black neighborhoods and the dissolution of the normal social fabric in the ghettoes. Moynihan cited white racism as a cause, but highlighted broken and female-led families as perpetuators of the current dilemma. Moynihan feared that the legacy of slavery and later oppression in the South had impaired the self-confidence of African-American males. It had weakened their position as heads-of-household, and led them to abandon their families.

Black Macho in itself might not merit major focus in the gender issue, but it become the center of a wide-ranging discussion and elicited some interesting viewpoints and perspectives that, to many in the black intellectual community, clearly needed attention. Thus, early on, some black feminists were marking off their concerns from those of white women. In some cases they made sharp differentiations and returned attention to the issues raised by the Moynihan Report. Elizabeth Hood, for example, wrote that the white feminist movement derived directly from the relationship of white women to white men. Feminism to white women essentially meant access to those positions of privilege long occupied by white men, she asserted. Those positions, furthermore, perpetuated the system of racism in America. Black women, by contrast, had no powerful male order to which they could aspire. They lacked economically able husbands and confronted, by necessity more than choice, the all-consuming challenge of heading a household. To illustrate the incompatibility of white and black feminism, Hood cited recent law suits in which white women sued universities on their policies of minority preference for black students.[52]

The gender question also provided another opening for black writers on the Left. They naturally found the source of the problem in capitalism. Angela Davis, who as noted recognized a problem, believed that the essence of black male maltreatment of women—rape—had its roots in the capitalist takeover of the South in the post-Civil War era. Working-class blacks, she reported, accepted a bribe: gain manliness through rape while remaining in their perpetuated state of class victimization. She offered but one formula for any surcease of this problem: "the threat of rape will exist as long as capitalist society survives."[53]

Black males had their say in the matter, too. Sociologist Robert Staples refuted Wallace. Indeed, his entry partly inspired the *Black Scholar* forum on this subject and engaged several women contributors specifically against *him*. Staples' edited book, *The Black Family: Essays and Studies* had appeared in 1971. Staples said that black women, capitalizing on their double minority status, were surpassing black men in education and economic achievement. This emergence of the "strong black woman" understandably, said Staples, threatens black men. Many do not stay with their families, for to the resentful black male "desertion is his form of masculine protest." Furthermore, Staples argued, some middle-class black males, with more choices available to them, turn to white women, who better fit the "model of femininity" they need. However much Staples tried to place the issue in perspective by suggesting that successful black men had simply internalized white social values, his words cut and black feminists perceived an afront.[54]

Staples believed he could undo Wallace by placing a Marxist accent on his case. With a bow to Mao Zedong for theoretical support, Staples proclaimed that the issue in question was neither racism nor sexism; instead, he appealed to the old chestnut, "monopoly capitalism." Wallace, he contended, failed to see the matter correctly because of her middle-class identity. That identity disabled her from understanding black working-class culture and from recognizing why black sexism flourishes within it. As capitalism deprived black men of economic power, Staples speculated, they embraced the symbols of manhood, sexual conquest, and dominance of women as their only recourse. Staples dismissed Wallace's unrevolutionary book as a species of neoconservatism.[55]

Other radical critiques of Wallace reflected a prevailing Marxist intellectual paradigm—its totalist epistemology. Pauline Stone believed that Wallace cast her presentation on gender too narrowly. Her "reformist feminism" reflected liberal-bourgeois habits of fragmenting the social whole and approaching an issue such as this one in a piecemeal manner. But the gender problem, Stone argued, would yield no solution apart from confrontation with the whole complexity of racist and capitalist America. Without these "links with the totality," Wallace's book, Stone charged, reduced the great revolutionary efforts of the 1960s to a "psychosexual drama" rooted in the neuroses of black men.[56]

The gender debate did indeed show that class perspective figured largely in black thought. Perhaps the class issue served to deflect attention from an unwelcome subject, but there was no denying that many wanted to make Wallace's middle-class standing a topic of its own. One black woman dismissed Wallace as the "darling of the *Ms.* crowd," locating her with white middle-class reformers and rendering her charges weightless.[57] A black writer took offense at Wallace's front-cover photographic portrait on *Ms.* and tied her to that magazine's "middle-class elitism," its pro-capitalism, and its white supremacism.[58] But having heard these dismissals made all too glibly, one black feminist, replying to Staples in particular, simply replied that no amount of capitalist injustice could legitimate the oppressive treatment of black women by black men.[59]

These considerations brought the discussion fully into a 1970s intellectual format, for as in other matters, the black gender issue raised the question of cultural constructions. Who constructs the culture? Who controls the narrative? What power interests emerge into clarity under deconstructive analysis? Distinguished social psychologist Alvin Poussaint of Harvard addressed black gender in these terms. He saw the Wallace controversy as a classic and familiar case of white cultural manipulation designed to keep blacks divided among themselves. In the information age the problem of image creation, he believed, becomes especially acute and he turned his critical eyes directly on "the white media." Wallace as black mattered less than Wallace as cover-girl on *Ms.,* establishment literary image-maker of the white media. Wrote Poussaint: "The images they present of black males are white racist stereotypes: violent, psychopathic, no-good, low-down irresponsible, savage sexual animals and potential rapists to boot." Poussaint did not find it surprising that white males and white feminists wanted to promote Wallace's book, and regretted that black women were validating the "carefully manufactured" constructs of black maleness, constructs that white society has always used to rationalize slavery, legal segregation, and disenfranchisement of blacks. And in the current women's liberation movement, "controlled by white middle-class females," the black male once again becomes scapegoat, victim of a carefully crafted image in an image-driven society.[60]

Debating black has always figured prominently in African-American culture. Recall the contrasting positions taken by Booker T. Washington and William E. B. Du Bois and later between Martin Luther King, Jr., and Malcolm X. The 1960s saw black intellectualism intrigued and hopeful about essentialist and monolithic notions of "black." But such constructions could not withstand the fracturing tendencies of the 1970s and black debate entered into a pluralistic era. Painful words sometimes induced angry responses. But black intellectual life acquired a greater candor and honesty as simplistic and holistic conceptions lost force, while diversity and complexity came to characterize the prevailing understanding of black America.

eight

Neoconservatism

The 1970s began with a moderate Republican president in the White House. They ended with a moderate Democrat occupying the Oval Office. These facts, of course, mislead with respect to the political transformation of the United States that occurred in this decade. Its first year saw a continuing wave of protest against American involvement in Vietnam and a continuing liberal agenda in Congress (eighteen-year-olds won the right to vote in national elections). But ten years later, America prepared to elect the most avowedly conservative president in the twentieth century, and Republicans, with many new, like-minded conservatives, captured the Senate for the first time since the early 1950s.

Our subject here is the political culture of the 1970s, and it raises several questions. What caused the electoral shift to conservatism in the United States and where can we locate the historical and cultural roots of that shift? What does the reemergence of conservatism tell us about the incidence of postindustrialism in American life, or, in other words, how might we understand the new conservatism in terms of the larger pattern of social and cultural change in the 1970s? Also, we need to take note of an impressive intellectual renaissance of conservatism. How did journalists and academics advance a new conservative critique of American society and politics? How did the "neoconservatives" in particular reflect the sociological transformations that prompted the political realignments in the 1970s, and how did this group, in fact, redefine conservatism?

Ostensibly, a new kind of conservatism did flourish in the 1970s and beyond. It did not spring from the traditionalism of agrarian elites or from the privileged leadership of corporate America. This conservatism had an insurgent quality about; it purported to speak for the mass of Americans poised against a liberal elite that disdained the habits and prejudices of the common people. Neoconservative writers, almost to a person, had once been committed Democrats, but they now saw their party captured by a new constituency. Their personal disaffection, indeed their sense of betrayal, found its voice in inveighing against the "New Class" of liberal leadership now ascendant in their party. Many became Republicans.

The allegedly "populist" character of the new conservatism raised the question whether this conservatism was truly new. Might it not have its antecedents in previous insurgent movements of the radical Right? Should these earlier movements be considered preparatory of the 1970s and might theories that explained them help us understand this latest phenomenon?

The anticommunist crusade led by Senator Joseph McCarthy of Wisconsin in the early 1950s certainly expressed populist and antielitist prejudices. His references to the "bright young men who are born with silver spoons in their mouths" expressed McCarthy's disdain for the State Department officials, often Ivy League graduates, whom he accused of Communist sympathies. "It has not been the less fortunate or members of minority groups who have been selling this nation out," McCarthy charged, "but rather those who have had all the benefits that the wealthiest nation on earth has to offer—the finest homes, the finest college education, and the finest jobs in Government we can give."[1]

The McCarthy experience produced extensive efforts to understand conservatism as a peculiar phenomenon in the United States. In particular, the essays collected in *The New American Right* (1955) looked back to the Populists of the previous century and invoked historian Richard Hofstadter's "status thesis" to explain a politics of resentment for both that earlier group and McCarthy's recent constituency. Populism, that thesis asserted, appealed to individuals uncertain of their place in American society and quick to imagine conspiratorial forces that caused their victimization. The thesis had limited use, but it is noteworthy that *The New American Right* did anticipate a shift of some consequence when it noted the prominence of third-generation white ethnic groups in the McCarthy constituency, a focus of attention in the new conservatism of the 1970s.[2]

Interpretations of McCarthy also tapped other themes that anticipate the later conservative movement. Some analysts saw McCarthy as voicing particularly anti-internationalist, or better, anticosmopolitan feelings. Historically, American politics has seen recurring expressions of provincial protest—anti-British feelings, hostility toward New York bankers and their internationalist money connections, or anti-Semitism. Communism had just this appearance of a foreign import, an alien presence, as to inflate the popular imagination about its sinister character. Anti-Communism, therefore, aroused the fears of individuals oriented toward their local culture and tribal connections and loyal to traditional moral, religious, and patriotic values. These loyalties often had clear political manifestations, and McCarthy, for one, spoke to an ongoing issue in the Republican party—the efforts of a Midwestern, conservative group to wrest control from an eastern, internationalist leadership.[3]

McCarthy found less popular appeal in the South, where his Catholicism may have handicapped him. It remained for George Wallace, then, to give the insurgent conservative movement at first a Southern, and then a larger, national resonance. Wallace, of course, won notoriety when, as governor, he defied the court-ordered desegregation of the University of Alabama in 1963. Wallace spoke for a white South determined to resist the civil rights movement, now almost a decade old. He may have earned his credentials as a lawyer, but he personified, too, the populist white South. He had been a Golden Gloves boxer, a cotton chopper, a truck driver, and he had married a dime-store clerk. Wallace challenged Lyndon Johnson in the Democratic primaries of 1964, but the Republicans persuaded him not to mount an independent party movement in the November election for fear of diminishing the conservative vote for Barry Goldwater. In 1968, however, Wallace went all out.

To bring his challenge to the national electorate, Wallace perceived astutely that he could do better than merely play the race card. He succeeded in giving his campaign a larger message by invoking an America divided between the ordinary, common citizens and a bureaucratic and intellectual elite determined to exercise its special agenda of reform. Wallace could outdo anyone in populist rhetoric. Hence, as he saw them, the "real issues" in America:

> Now what are the real issues that exist today in these United States? It is the trend of pseudo-intellectual government, where a select, elite group have written guidelines in bureaus and court decisions, have spoken from some pulpits, some college campuses, some newspaper offices, looking down their noses at the average man on the street, *the glassworker, the steelworker, the autoworker, and the textile worker, the farmer, the policeman, the beautician, and the barber, and the little businessman,* saying to him that you do not know how to get up in the morning or to go to bed at night unless we write you a guideline. . . .[4]

Wallace provides additional significance for the emerging conservative movement. His surprising successes in the early Democratic primaries in 1968 (34 percent of the vote in Wisconsin; 30 percent in Indiana; 43 percent in Maryland) showed him capturing a Democratic voting group that would soon gravitate in great numbers to the Republican party. Significantly, Wallace supporters in Indiana tended to identify themselves as working class, rather than middle class, the affiliation named by supporters of rivals Hubert Humphrey and Richard Nixon.[5] Wallace advanced a populist message far more focused on cultural and social issues than on economic ones. The populism that once denounced the powerful trusts and corporations, the Wall Street bankers and the big commercial interests, now hardly noticed the economic situation of the lower classes and certainly had no prescription for their material improvement. Wallace instead spoke to America's island communities and subcultures that saw themselves besieged by what one historian has labeled "an unholy trinity of federal officials, cosmopolitan intellectuals, and militant blacks." Therein lay some political lessons for the new conservatives.[6]

The shifting political alignments of the 1960s held a particular interest for political theorist Kevin P. Phillips. And Phillips' books, *The Emerging Republican Majority* (1969) and *Mediacracy* (1975) have a particular interest for us because Phillips acted not only as interpreter of the new electoral patterns but as advocate of the new conservative insurgency of the late 1960s and 1970s. Phillips served the Nixon administration as voting patterns analyst for the candidate's campaign manager, John Mitchell. His studies led to the publication of *Republican Majority*, a major document of the conservative movement.

Phillips' book offered exhaustive statistical analysis—143 charts and 47 maps—a microstudy of voting trends going back many decades. Phillips described a political *evolution* in the United States, an emerging new paradigm in the two-party system, "the beginning of a new era in American politics." The new politics was changing the meaning of "liberal" and "conservative," Phillips believed. It had something to do with social class, but not in the traditional understanding of the term. The new politics had something to do with economics, but not much. It had far more to do with ethnic and cultural matters, now the key fault lines in American society. "Everywhere," Phillips wrote, "ethnic, regional and cultural loyalties constitute the principal dynamics of American voting."[7]

What led Phillips to describe a major transformation in American politics? His study surveyed the nation by looking at four geographical regions, beginning with the key area of the Northeast (New England plus New York, Pennsylvania, New Jersey, Maryland, and Delaware). This region, Phillips argued, had become the locus of a new liberal Establishment, one that reflected the successful institutionalization of the New Deal over a half-century. Its power and political interests had emerged in part through its connections with the extended federal government, the primary legacy of the New Deal. Phillips wrote: "A new Establishment—the media, universities, conglomerate corporations, research and development corporations—has achieved much of the power of the industrial and financial establishment dethroned by the New Deal. This new Establishment thrives on a government vastly more powerful than that developed by the business titans of the Nineteen-Thirties."[8]

What had once been the bastions of conservatism—the "silk stocking districts" of the cities and the suburbs—were now trending liberal. Phillips saw this departure in the Goldwater debacle of 1964, where the conservative Republican suffered his party's largest decline from its previous loyalties in precisely these areas. Likewise did George Wallace have his worst showing in New England. At the same time other groups began to trend conservative—the urban Italian and Irish, rural non-Yankees, new suburbanites (including many ethnic Catholics, lower-income Jews, milltowners)—many of them once solidly in the New Deal coalition. These constituencies formed the vanguard of what Phillips labeled "popular conservatism." Indeed, *Republican Majority* exudes its author's own populist rhetoric, denoted by his ready references to "silk-stocking" urbanites, the "knowledge industry," "conglomerate corporatism," and "dollar internationalism." Nor were there undisguised in Phillips the anti-intellectual overtones so pronounced among populist neoconservatives. Keynoting the liberal Democratic trend, he said, were "the research directors, associate professors, social workers, educational consultants, urbanologists, development planners, journalists . . . communications specialists, culture vendors . . . poverty theorists and so forth."[9]

Phillips carried his analysis into the other regions of the country—the South, the Heartland, and the Pacific States. His precise statistical evidence enabled him to avoid easy generalities, as he elaborated the subtleties that differentiated regions, states, and cities, but they did point to the same persistent trend—a conservative, Republican insurgency among white, and especially ethnic white, America in the middle and lower income levels, and the gravitation of other whites—more affluent, located in older suburbs or in "fashionable" city wards—to the Democrats. Within a few years Phillips more precisely explained these patterns under the encompassing theme of post-industrial shift.

In the meantime, the 1970s began to witness a new, visible element of the New Right. You could see some signs of the change around the very campuses that had been the loci of the youth counterculture and the angry protests against status quo politics. The students had the same bedraggled clothing— the young men sported the same long hair and beards, and the women wore the familiar peasant dresses. But this group did not seek the redemption of the world through politics and reform. They did not paper their bedrooms with the iconography of Che or Mao. These new disciples looked inward. They sought personal salvation in a very ancient source and they preached a very simple message. They were the "Jesus Freaks."

The "Jesus Freaks" movement registered a changing mood in America. Disillusionment with sixties culture settled slowly on the nation. The Left was cracking up. The August 1970 bombing at the University of Wisconsin in Madison, causing the death of a young researcher, induced sobering second thoughts on thousands of advocates or practitioners of the Deed. SDS had dissolved in 1969 into meaningless but furious ideological divisions, announcing its total irrelevance to everything. Political acts became missions of suicide as the frenzied "Weatherman" faction of the Left blew itself up making home-made bombs. Communal retreats, the utopian promise of the counterculture, revealed their potentially horrible, ugly side in the Manson murders of 1969. The path to a world of love and peace seemed paved with violence and destruction. Redemption by politics lost its lustre. So too did the drug culture, as overdoses took the lives of famous rock stars. For many, drugs showed not an inner life of calm and self-awareness but a hellish trip to oblivion.

Had the religious message of the Jesus people become the dominant religious strain in the 1970s, it might have had a calming effect on the overheated political culture of the nation. But the religious news that most captured the attention of the American public, and of historians and commentators, told a different story. The religious revival of the 1970s centered in an evangelical awakening. American history, to be sure, had long been witness to such movements, and indeed, evangelical Protestantism had been a dominant, shaping force of American culture and politics in the nineteenth century. And the new revival had familiar markings. It stressed spiritual rebirth, as "born-again Christianity" became a cultural label of the 1970s, exemplified by one of its confessors, President Jimmy Carter. The evangelical revival also exercised a traditional methodology—the use of the most available media for its outreach. Indeed, the "electronic pulpit," flooding the air waves of radio and television, reached audiences of millions of people, with incoming dollars to match. Billy Graham pioneered this effort in the 1950s and now individuals such as Jimmy Swaggart, Oral Roberts, Jim Bakker, and Pat Robertson created a corporate religious conglomerate in the United States.

None more shaped the dominant image of the evangelical revival in the 1970s, however, than Jerry Falwell. For Falwell, though he had once refused to see any political message in Christianity, now brought it into the political maelstrom of the decade. He added to politics another cultural input. From his operational base at the Thomas Road Baptist Church in Lynchburg, Virginia, where Falwell's "Old-Time Gospel Hour" had become a $57 million industry by decade's end, this television preacher issued his battle cry to secular America.

Falwell preached anti-Communism; he decried the moral sin of abortion; he attacked pornography; he rejected homosexuals' demands for civil rights; and he cast his lot with Phyllis Schlafly in an all-out effort to defeat the Equal Rights Amendment and the feminist agenda. Falwell gave his message a large universal theme: all the problems that beset America—its violence, its decaying moral standards, and, above all, its threatened family structure—derived from a turn from traditional Christianity and a lapse into secular humanism. As Timothy Dwight at Yale College once warned against the corrosive inroads of the "Bavarian Illuminati," so did Falwell portray a sinister, corrupting force—"secular humanism"—that eroded American vitality and national purpose. Only inner rebirth, the rediscovery of Christ, could save America from a terrible decay and disintegration, Falwell preached. In 1979, Falwell organized the movement he called the Moral Majority. On board were some major political activists of the New Right.[10]

Religion now had fully entered the communications age. By decade's end, no less than three hundred radio stations, thirty-six television stations, and three networks offered full-time religious programming. Insofar as they took on political advocacy, too, their messages coincided directly with the New Right agenda.[11] Evangelical churches continued to grow in membership in the

1970s as the older "main-line" Protestant denominations—Episcopalian, United Church of Christ, Presbyterian, Methodist—declined in numbers.[12] Private schools, usually under evangelical auspices, were educating 1.5 million children at the end of the 1970s (and not simply because their parents wished to avoid racially integrated schools). Of course, we should not view evangelicalism as wholly related to right-wing politics. (Millions of black American evangelicals had no affinity for the Right's agenda.) Nor is it at all conclusive how the revival actually affected political voting in 1976 or 1980. Jimmy Carter won key southern states with evangelicals' votes. But clearly a counter-countercultural movement was afoot. Many received its messages and many acted on them, some at the voting booth, some at their local schools and in their town halls.

As noted, the emergence of the evangelical right reinforced a growing conservative insurgency and gave American politics more the appearance of a *kulturkampf*. When Kevin Phillips surveyed the political situation in the middle of the 1970s, he had reason to reinforce the thesis of his 1969 book. Interestingly, Phillips could now draw on a new historical scholarship forging significant new interpretations in the 1970s. A new group of scholars had been asserting that religious-ethnic-cultural differences had always been key influences in American politics, and in American political party identification especially. This "new political history," or "cultural politics" used extensive quantitative analysis (essentially statistical studies of voting patterns) to reach remarkably consistent conclusions.

In reaction to a generation of historians in the 1960s who emphasized economic classes and their attending patterns of exploitation, the new political history drew a more complex picture. It was distinctively non-Marxist in its conclusions. Voting patterns, it discovered, cut across class lines and revealed a different fault-line: "pietistic" Protestants, who charged politics with a moral-reformist dimension (temperance, antislavery, sabbatarianism) and "liturgical" Christians, who pursued religious salvation within the institutional churches, which churches also protected their folkways from the perceived moral imperialism of their rivals. These contrasting patterns, it was argued, provided the Whig-Republican (pietistic) and Democratic (liturgical) divisions in American politics. In some cases, cultural politics took note of other influences—manners, fashions, speech, drinking preferences— "lifestyle" behavior, in short. Thus, one could locate a certain Anglophile quality among Whigs, described by their clothing, manner of speech, love of English literature, and generally, their faith in the civilizing promise of English culture. Democrats, on the other hand, preferred the rough, earthy, commonstock character of provincial and folkish America.[13]

Phillips found the new scholarship informative for his 1975 book, *Mediacracy: American Parties and Politics in the Communications Age*. This book has a special interest for our study because Phillips now sought to give his 1969 study a more inclusive thesis. He found the key to America's changing political habits in its emerging "postindustrial" character. "Too little attention and analysis," Phillips wrote in his preface, "have been devoted to the political impact of a Postindustrial, or Communications Revolution, which appears to be as far reaching a phenomenon as the Industrial Revolution."[14] Phillips acknowledged a special debt to sociologist Daniel Bell in applying a postindustrial analysis to his subject.

The 1972 presidential election informed much of Phillips' discussion. We note two symbolic facts that he found especially illuminating. Item One: the Harvard Law School, in a straw poll, backed Democrat George McGovern, the most left-leaning presidential candidate from a major party in the twentieth century, six to one against Republican incumbent Richard Nixon. Item Two: Mississippi—the country's most impoverished state, the least cultured, the least educated—gave the Democratic candidate the lowest percentage of all the states, and this, for the fourth presidential election in a row. Massachusetts—near the top among the states in wealth, education, and culture—was the only state won by George McGovern. These results confirmed the trends that Phillips had earlier described. Now he sought a more precise thesis to explain them.

Chapter Two of *Mediacracy* offered a lengthy description of "PostIndustrial Society." It recounted a now familiar landscape: a new economic system, and new population centers, built increasingly around the sale of services and knowledge rather than manufactured products, and the declining populations of the older industrial cities and mill towns. Thus, Lowell, Massachusetts revealed its ghostly shells of a departed textile economy, while nearby Boston's Route 128 flourished with its research, think-tanks, and high-technology complexes. Phillips described this new postindustrial scene: "the huge bureaucracies of government multiplied tenfold since the New Deal era, the colleges and universities now serving 10 million young Americans, the huge communications empires, the network of think tank and charitable foundations, and the huge corporate giants of knowledge technology—IBM, Xerox, and so forth."[15]

Simply put, for Phillips, those most connected to the defining institutions of postindustrial society constituted the new liberal elite in American politics. To be sure, Phillips, in contrast to some neoconservative intellectuals who inveighed indiscriminately against the "New Class," recognized that certain components of the postindustrial complex did not move in its liberalizing direction—those involved in aerospace and military research, for example. But why, in general, a liberal trend? For one thing, Phillips asserted, the new postindustrial elite did not sell manufactured goods; it trafficked in, and thrived in a marketplace of ideas and information, where newness and change were its very *raison d'etre*. Wrote Phillips: "Instead of having a vested interest in stability, as did previous conservative business establishments, the knowledge sector has a vested interest in change—in the unmooring of convention, in socioeconomic experiments, in the ongoing consumption of new ideas."

Furthermore, Phillips believed, the communications industry effected a definitive connection to the liberal adversary culture. Magazines such as *Time* and *Newsweek*, and Eastern city papers such as the *New York Times*, the *Washington Post*, the *Boston Globe*, and the *Baltimore Sun*, became distinctly more liberal than the country as a whole. This postindustrial elite was clearly less tradition-oriented than its predecessor elites.[16]

The liberal political connection first became visible in two ways, Phillips showed. Beginning in the 1950s, several Democratic "reform" movements organized in the big cities. Spearheaded by middle-class professionals, and often flourishing as reform "clubs," they concentrated in the more fashionable locations of the cities and sought to dislocate the city machines from their working-class, ethnic connections, the perceived sources of their corruption.[17] Second, the Great Society programs of the 1960s turned government into a dynamic growth industry and spawned new connections to the knowledge industry: education, urban planning, social research, poverty studies, and more. By 1972, Phillips reported, 13.6 million people worked in federal, state, and local government positions. Bureaucracy, he noted, had become one of the largest segments of the United States economy, hiring more people than the entire durable-goods segment of manufacturing. It formed one component of "liberalism's multibillion-dollar social engineering industry."[18]

By 1975, however, Phillips could point to more signs of a continuing conservative reaction. In addition to the voting trends analyzed in his 1969 book, Phillips cited a general cultural disillusionment with the pretensions of the liberal elite—disaffection with the results of the high-tech, expert-run war in Vietnam and the failure of the Great Society programs to deliver on their grand and utopian promises. He further described an ethnic revival, including folk fairs and heritage studies, that gave a special emphasis to family, neighborhood, and community, and all resistant to the notion that America constituted a grand melting pot amenable to rational socioeconomic planning. He observed also the religious revival, especially active as part of the conservative insurgency in those areas that had once constituted the strength of the Populists and Democratic party—the South and West, and small-town America generally. Thus there continued the great reversal in American politics.[19]

The parallel intellectual movement in conservatism represented something of a reversal, too. The 1970s offered something new to the political lexicon in America, the term "neoconservatism." And yet, the word had that amorphous quality about it that described so much of the feel of postindustrial life. It did not appear until the latter part of the decade and seemed to suggest only that a new kind of conservative outlook had come into being. In fact, the neoconservative movement dates back at least to the middle 1960s. But if "neo" conservatism suggested a revised or a new conservatism, it was not clear that its practitioners intended any particular continuity with an older tradition. Was neoconservatism, then, just a new style? Or should it be called new because its advocates had backgrounds often strikingly different from other conservative intellectuals? To add to the confusion, most writers labeled as neoconservatives abjured that identification, and, in the judgment of other self-consciously conservative thinkers, the neoconservatives were not authentic conservatives at all.

Movement conservatives who decried the sinister power of a liberal elite effectively forged what one author has called a conservative "counter-establishment."[20] They created new conservative journals—*The Public Interest, The American Spectator* (originally the *Alternative*), *The National Interest*. In one case, they took over an established liberal publication—*Commentary.* They organized their own policy-oriented "think-tanks"—the American Enterprise Institute, the Heritage Foundation. And however much conservatives charged a *trahison des clercs* among the elite universities of the country, prominent neoconservative intellectuals could be found from Harvard to Berkeley as the intellectual insurgency advanced in the 1970s.

The neoconservatives especially gained attention. The most noted and notorious of them were journalists, not academics, their weapons of choice the short, biting essay, not the learned treatise. Critics called them street fighters, rough and combative, reflecting their beginnings in the city streets of New York. They made up for their want of metaphysical principles and first truths with a keen eye for the quotidian realities of things. They wrote to change policy and shunned the saintly unconcern for power affected by the conservative purists who denounced them.

To an old conservative Right committed to Christian principles and the Western intellectual tradition derived from them, the secular Jewish prevalence among the neoconservatives rankled. Nonetheless, the Jewish contributors gave neoconservatism its special traits and helped define its major issues. The case of Norman Podhoretz is illustrative. Podhoretz twice wrote his autobiography. *Making It*, in 1967, told, boastfully, of a Jewish boy born in New York in 1930, a precocious kid whose school teacher, "Mrs. K," called him a "filthy slum child," but bought him a suit of clothes so that he could cut a good figure for his Harvard interview. Podhoretz, however, continued his education at Columbia and Oxford, immersing himself in the literature of Western humanism, to the neglect of his Judaic rearing.[21] At the age of only thirty, Podhoretz in 1960 became editor of *Commentary* magazine, the major Jewish journal of political and cultural opinion. He resolved to make *Commentary* more leftist and now described himself as a "radical."

Podhoretz believed himself a forerunner of the nascent radical movement of the 1960s and he merged *Commentary* with that agenda into the early 1970s. But then came another turnabout, a move to the right that Podhoretz recounted in his book of 1979, *Breaking Ranks*. What had made a Jewish neoconservative out of this man of the Left? For one, Podhoretz had never accepted the counterculture whole hog. He had not taken a liking to the Beat Culture of the 1950s nor had he joined other intellectuals—conservative and liberal—in fashionable disaffection with middle-class life in the United States. He disdained the commercial hustlers who tried to make money off the 1960s' counterculture—"rock stars, publishing tycoons, drug dealers, and other enterprising entrepreneurs." He charged that those comfortable Americans who bought into the counterculture exercised a smug moral superiority over others. They dismissed the hard work of ordinary Americans as crude materialism. They celebrated peace and love against competition and credited themselves with caring and compassion amid the lesser benevolence of others. Particularly when the pacifist ethic threatened to disabuse Americans of the Communist threat did Podhoretz raise his voice in protest.[22]

In a sense, Podhoretz never left the Jewish ghetto celebrated in *Making It*. His neoconservatism was a street-tough animosity toward the gilded, establishment Left that bred the counterculture. Something offended him in its chic and easy radicalism. It rang inauthentic. He pointed to the liberal suburbanites who championed racial integration at no cost to themselves or their children. He denounced the "safe" detractors of the Vietnam War, intellectuals who risked nothing in sheltered academia. Podhoretz wholly registered neoconservative disdain for the "New Class," and his language, too, reverberated with the populist rhetoric employed against this elite. He described "an aggression by a new and rapidly growing group of prosperous and well-educated people calling themselves liberals against a less prosperous and less well-educated combination of groups, mostly in the working and lower middle classes." His essay "The Adversary Culture and the New Class" sounded this neoconservative theme with special vigor.[23]

In such sentiments as these, the intellectual movement in conservatism touched the political. The 1970s witnessed an accelerated shift in the patterns of class and social group in the two-party system. After 1968, the Democrats, at the prompting of their insurgent left wing, moved to a quota system in their delegate selection process for presidential conventions, one designed to increase the representation of minorities and women. The party thus broke emphatically with its leadership base of labor unions, big city mayors, and a large ethnic constituency. In reaction, traditional-minded Democrats, including Podhoretz, his wife Midge Decter, Jeane Kirkpatrick, Ben Wattenberg, and Daniel Patrick Moynihan, formed the Committee for a Democratic Majority to recover that base and dissociate their party from its prevailing "antibourgeois attitudes."[24]

But, as E. J. Dionne, Jr., points out, these changes produced a different Democratic party. "Over the long run," he writes, "the new party rules . . . led to an increasing role for the well-to-do and a declining role for the working and middle classes," especially as the new women representatives came from these ranks. They had the effect of "concentrating power into the hands of a culturally 'advanced' upper middle class."[25] Furthermore, the demographic shifts that Phillips described brought to Washington, in the "Class of '74," a "New Democrat"—congressmen elected disproportionately from middle-class and suburban areas. This group carried more of a cultural agenda than an economic one, in contrast to the old New Deal Democrats. And issues such as feminism, favored by this group, put them increasingly at odds with lower-class women.[26]

Another Jewish voice also elaborated neoconservative principles. Nathan Glazer, a Jewish sociologist at Harvard, gave neoconservatism a more precise intellectual content. Born in New York City in 1923, Glazer graduated from City College and earned higher degrees at Pennsylvania and Columbia. His career combined journalism and academics. He served on the editorial staff of *Commentary* for eight years after 1945 and was a coauthor of David Riesman's celebrated book of 1950, *The Lonely Crowd*. He taught at the University of California at Berkeley in the 1960s and then joined the Harvard faculty. He became coeditor of *The Public Interest* in 1973.

Glazer, too, had long considered himself a radical. But in 1970 he asked this question of himself: "How does a radical—a mild radical, it is true . . . in the 1960s—end up by early 1970 as a conservative, a mild conservative, but still closer to those who now call themselves conservatives than to those who call themselves liberal?"[27] Glazer began to change politically at Berkeley. The free speech movement of 1964 and afterward marked the symbolic beginning of the student movement of that decade. Some liberals hoped to see the movement expand into a wider attack on the major institutions of American society and they believed they saw in the students a welcome idealism. But Glazer and other liberals reacted more cautiously. They perceived in the student protests the signs of irrationalism, and a mood of intolerance, even a totalitarian mentality. Later Glazer would see in the New Left a nihilistic assault on the social fabric that rendered vulnerable the fragile institutions of liberal, democratic society. Glazer now expressed concern for the order, authority, and equilibrium necessary for the functioning of a free nation. In this concern he echoed familiar conservative sentiments.[28]

As Glazer expanded his critique of 1970s liberalism, one issue, high among the concerns of all conservatives, became paramount. Neoconservatives liked to argue that it was not they who had changed in the 1970s; liberalism had changed. In particular, they argued, liberalism had shifted from a concern for equality of opportunity to equality of results, to a politics of statistical parity, in short. Glazer portrayed government programs of school busing for racial integration and the new Affirmative Action directives as the sinister manifestations of the new liberalism. In 1975 he published *Affirmative Discrimination*. In the neoconservative style, the book compiled an array of statistics, but did not hesitate to register moral judgments as well. Glazer condemned government policies that took account of race and sex in education and employment as the near equivalent of the Nuremberg Laws of Nazi Germany. He resented liberal patronizing of allegedly "helpless" minorities. He judged the new liberalism a threat to freedom. "The tone of civil rights cases," he wrote, "has turned from one in which the main note is the expansion of freedom into one in which the main note is the imposition of restrictions." And an America defined legally by statistical groups, Glazer argued, defied any notion of genuine community. The rationalism of liberal legalism conspired against America's authentic, rich diversity.[29]

Neoconservatism received its most powerful expression from Irving Kristol. Indeed, he won the nickname "Godfather of Neoconservatism" and rejoiced at the nomination. He was born in Brooklyn in 1920 to a family with Jewish roots in Eastern Europe. Kristol remembered a grandfather steeped in rabbinic learning, and his own parents observed the high religious holidays and honored kosher practices. His education at City College placed Kristol in the intellectual genealogy of the "New York Intellectuals." Here the bright, young, and mostly Jewish men of the city sharpened their political wits in ideological debates that posed Stalinists against Trotskyists. Kristol joined the youth group of the latter and after graduation followed his leftist leanings into the Young People's Socialist League. He remarked, however, that he got his best education, and his most exciting, from reading the quarterly issues of *Partisan Review*, America's pioneering journal in leftist politics and cultural modernism.[30]

Going into the 1960s, Kristol could still regard himself as a good liberal Democrat. He shared the party's dominant anticommunism and its commitment to preserving and extending the basic New Deal program of reform. But increasingly over the decade his loyalties eroded. In the campaign efforts of both Eugene McCarthy and Robert Kennedy in 1968, Kristol saw a dangerous turn to the left that estranged the party from its traditional constituency. When the party chose George McGovern as its presidential candidate in 1972, Kristol saw a wholesale sellout to the party's undemocratic left wing. He became a Republican, and he said of this change, "in order to become a neoconservative all you had to do was stand in place."[31]

Kristol's move should have surprised no one, for it had been a long time brewing. In 1965, he and Daniel Bell had introduced *The Public Interest*, a journal of sociology and economics, mostly, that sought to put the liberal agenda to the hardest empirical tests. It was patented neoconservatism. It relied for its suasion not so much on religious dogma or metaphysical truth but on the quantitative methodologies of the academic social sciences. Contributors presented their analyses in statistics-laden studies, scrutinizing government policies in education, urban renewal, housing, taxation, and other worldly endeavors. They did not offer doomsday scenarios, but brought sober judgments against the great hopes and redemptory expectations of 1960s liberalism.[32] Neoconservatives, looking at the array of social problems that beset the nation, concluded that many were simply intractable and that no amount of government largesse could alleviate them. They spoke of a dysfunctional "under class" of individuals incapable of any productive social roles. In its 1974 special issue, *The Public Interest* presented "The Great Society: Lessons for the Future." Those lessons derived from the failures of the past. As Kristol was so often quoted as saying: a neoconservative was a liberal who has been mugged by reality.

If neoconservatives wished to give the public sector a little reality therapy, the most discerning of them also expressed ambiguities about capitalism and the free market economic system. Here, too, Kristol most effectively described the problem. Like many neoconservatives Kristol endorsed capitalism, but not out of any genuine passion for it. He accepted capitalism because it worked. Of all economic arrangements it most effectively answered human, material wants. Socialism, one of the great and noble ideas in Western thinking, now lay in ruin, Kristol said. It remained the property only of utopians and dictators, and those who just could not accept the democratic fact of a market economy, where people vote with their pocketbooks.[33]

Why, then, Kristol's quarrel with capitalism? He wanted to distinguish first between capitalism as an economic system and capitalism as a moral system. Capitalism, Kristol explained, orients individuals to the marketplace; it is a system for the enhancement of material well-being. The bourgeois ethic (or what historians sometimes call the "Protestant ethic") orients people toward themselves; it is a means for regulating, or indeed moderating, the innate drives of individuals toward pleasure, toward the enjoyment of those material acquisitions that capitalism supplies abundantly. The capitalist ethic, said Kristol, is an ethic of freedom; the bourgeois ethic is an ethic of control, of self-discipline, above all of delayed gratifications. And it is the bourgeois ethic that gives capitalism its legitimacy, he believed. It made capitalism something more than a corollary of materialism or hedonism. For a long time this alliance of the two ethics had worked well, he believed. Wealth and material success roughly approximated the degree of personal virtue in those who amassed them. Capitalism, Kristol wrote, "had a genuine relation to the individual as a moral person. One acquired riches by being honest, diligent, prudent, pious, and fortunate."[34]

But Kristol confronted a problem in this relationship, one anticipated by economists such as Joseph Schumpeter and addressed with acuteness by Daniel Bell in his 1974 book *The Cultural Contradictions of Capitalism*, previously considered. The problem was the estrangement of capitalism from the moral system—the bourgeois ethic— that legitimated it. For capitalism, in its material successes, created a climate in which the demand for the immediate enjoyment of its fruits proved irresistible. The inner self-discipline that marked the bourgeois personality, said Kristol, succumbed increasingly to a culture, a capitalist culture, that forsook all self-discipline and yielded to an imagination of indefinite material gratification. Parents who by hard work and postponed pleasures gained affluence had a difficult time passing on their good habits to their progeny, born into that affluence. Advertising, too, with its message that anyone could purchase the necessities of a good life, conspired against this effort. To someone like Kristol who remembered the economic poverty of his Jewish youth, where, he said, to buy now and pay later was a sign of personal weakness and moral turpitude, the contemporary credit culture of the United States signified national degeneration.[35]

In 1972, Kristol had become a regular contributor to the *Wall Street Journal.* But he showed no shyness in levying his moral censure against the very power brokers of American capitalism in his midst. For one of the culprits in America's declining public culture, Kristol insisted, was American business itself. Business, he lamented, knew no value except the bottom line. In the 1960s and 1970s, Kristol asserted, the contradictions of capitalism reached their absurd height when American business bought into the counterculture itself. It traded in the very commodities—books, records, movies, clothes— that were disseminating the antibusiness, antibourgeois culture of the Left. Those on the left, of course, called this process "co-optation." Kristol called it a sellout. Capitalism had arrived at the point where the singular measure of profit reigned; it could muster no moral or ideological resistance to the hedo- nistic, libertarian ethos of America.[36] Lenin once said that the rope on which he hung the capitalists would be one that he had bought from them.

Neoconservatism came into being as America experienced the transition to postindustrialism. Much of its political fury derived from the new sociological arrangements of that condition, especially the power shifts represented by the despised "New Class." But neoconservatism shared with other conservative expressions a restorative motif, an effort to abate, or undo, the sense of weightlessness, even of disintegration, in postindustrial conditions. Kristol longed for the solidarity of bourgeois society and its older values, however much he found bourgeois society "prosaic" and generally uninspiring, lacking in heroic virtues. But now he looked at a vulgar world of merely pecuniary values, a society morally adrift, anchorless. Other conservatives, as will be dis- cussed, pursued the restorative effort along different lines. They wished to recover a sense of place, of community, of heritage; when all seemed to be yielding to liberalism's rationalism, they looked for kinship ties, for human relations blood-rich and thick, as their points of resistance.

When Michael Novak published his book *The Rise of the Unmeltable Ethnics* in 1972, he was completing a sojourn on the Left. *Unmeltable Ethnics* marked his mid-point in a transition to neoconservatism, and indeed by the end of the decade Novak had become the most prominent Catholic of that persuasion. Much of his writing to date had dealt with Church issues, but they often led to political translations that Novak himself carried into the radical politics of the sixties, including especially protests against the war in Vietnam. *Unmeltable Ethnics* reflects his career on the Left, but it also bears the markings of a conservative complaint now becoming familiar in the 1970s.

Novak subtitled his book *Politics and Culture in the Seventies.* In words that echoed the New Left, he began by describing an America beset by an oppres- sive political and moral culture, a rationalist strait-jacket that threatened to suffocate every genuine human passion and spontaneity. He saw American individualism become hollow and meaningless, depriving its citizens of the bonds of fellowship, family, and tribal intimacy. But Novak did not look to intellectuals to show the way out, nor did he hail a rebellious youthful genera- tion. He looked instead to America's ethnic groups, especially those he dubbed the PIGS—the Poles, Italians, Greeks, and Slavs.

The recent civil rights movement in the United States had defined "two Americas"—one black, one white; feminists described another America— one male, one female. Novak employed a similar dualism, but this one marked off the world of the Anglo-Saxon from the world of the ethnics. And he described two very different worlds.

The southern and eastern European immigrants, Novak believed, brought to the United States a worldly sense that left them wholly outside the Lock- ean rational and individualistic universe of the English and northern Euro- pean groups. For the people whom Novak called the WASPs had a dominant trait—an individualism that fed off the boundlessness and openness of early American life and valued a material progress born of individual drive and ambition. At the same time, however, the Anglo-Saxon bore a rationalist com- pulsion to control and order things, to impose discipline and organization on nature, on public life, and on his own inner being. And on all that he touched, wrote Novak, the WASP sought to assert a moral order. This particular com- bination of freedom and control, said Novak, gave Anglo-Saxon America its special psychic character.[37]

Ethnic culture, by contrast, was blood-rich, thriving on the enduring bonds of family and kinship ties. Ethnic consciousness did not project onto the world the image of a new order or even of a society transformed. It pursued no new moral universes, no politics of purification. Novak saw in the ethnics a culture of earthiness, a naturalism accepting of the world and its evils. But the immigrant bearers of this culture—warm-hearted, passionate—ran smack into the cool, clean, controlled world of the Yankee. "Immigrants from south- ern and eastern Europe," Novak wrote, "had to learn order, discipline, neat- ness, cleanliness, reserve. They had to learn to modulate emotion, to control passion, to hold their hands still, to hold the muscles of their face placid, to find food and body odors offensive, to quieten their voices, to present them- selves as coolly reasonable."[38]

Anglo-Saxonism, said Novak, secured its grip on the rest of America through its control of the corporate headquarters that ran the capitalist sys- tem. But Novak also highlighted another elite. Chapter Five of *Unmeltable Eth- nics* has the title "The Intellectuals of the Northeast." In the universities, espe- cially in the elite eastern universities, Novak located the ethic of the Enlightenment, the cult of reason and skepticism and an attending disdain for the traditional values and the habits of ordinary people. He described also a growing hostility toward such people and toward its politics. When in 1973, Vice President Agnew (Spiro Theodore Anagnostopoulos, son a Greek immi- grant) lashed out against the student radicals ("an effete group of impudent snobs"), Novak believed he saw an old culture war taking on new form.[39]

151

Novak's sympathies once tied him to the New Left. Indeed, in 1972, he still spoke its language:

> We may also see in the youth culture [of today] a profound starvation for a denser family life, a richer life of the senses, the instincts, the memory. No other group of young people in history was ever brought up under a more intensive dose of value-free discourse, quantification, analytic rationality, meritocratic competition, universal standards (IQ, College Boards). What was almost wholly neglected in their upbringing was the concrete, emotive, even tribal side of human nature. To that they were drawn in a desperate way, like air sucked into a vacuum. Music, dress, sound, light, and feeling ran into the farthest extreme from industrial, suburban rationality.[40]

Nonetheless, *Unmeltable Ethnics* carried Novak on a course toward neoconservatism. For one thing, the moral-rationalist politics that he disdained he now located in the reformist political tradition of America, shaped, he believed, by a puritanical, Yankee quest to make the world over, to purge it of sin, to save all reluctant souls. Reformers saw the world, he said, as so many machine parts, needing only to be retooled for more efficient coordination and function. The reformers' democracy, he charged, was a "soulless" mass society constituted by the quantifying process and norms of public opinion polls. The ethnic revolt, in turn, promised a new, more genuine democracy of "the people."[41]

Increasingly in the 1970s, Novak came to identify the New Left itself as the heritor of the WASP political tradition. And increasingly he denounced it for its utopianism, for its moral rigidity and self-righteousness, for its sense of superiority and arrogance, and especially for its politics of guilt. Throughout the decade Novak maintained his loyalties to the Democratic party, but with waning enthusiasm. After the debacle of 1972 he joined with other disaffected Democrats to form the Committee for a Democratic Majority, committed, as noted, to retrieving the party from the New Class elites that had pirated it from its genuine constituencies.[42]

The unspoken secret about *Unmeltable Ethnics* is just this: you did not have to be one of the PIGS to identity with its thesis. *Unmeltable Ethnics* was an allegory of a changing America. Despite the precise nomenclature Novak employed, his book essentially portrayed a nation more and more divided between a rationalist culture controlled by a liberal elite, and the array of ordinary Americans with their own quotidian hopes and ambitions. In 1978, in an essay he called "A Changed View," Novak described, on the one hand, the new liberal cohort, born of affluent parents and products of elite universities, young professionals in law, education, and the media, zealous to change America by their progressive agenda. On the other hand, he described a commonfolk majority, the democratic majority, who drank beer and watched foot-